THIS BOOK BELONGS TO:

CONTACT INFORMATION	
NAME:	
ADDRESS:	
PHONE:	

START / END DATES

___ / ___ / ___   TO   ___ / ___ / ___

DEDICATION

This Pool Maintenance Log Journal is dedicated to all the pool owners out there who want to track their pool maintenance and document their findings in the process.

You are my inspiration for producing books and I'm honored to be a part of keeping all of your Pool Maintenance notes and records organized.

This journal notebook will help you record your details about your swimming pool.

Thoughtfully put together with these sections to record: Check List, Items Purchased, Items Needed To Purchase, Notes & Further Observations Sections, Daily Inspection Record, Bi-Hourly Water Tests.

HOW TO USE THIS BOOK

The purpose of this book is to keep all of your Pool Maintenance notes all in one place. It will help keep you organized.

This Pool Maintenance Log Book will allow you to accurately document every detail about maintaining your swimming pool. It's a great way to chart your course through a healthy pool. Here are examples of the prompts for you to fill in and write about your experience in this book:

1. Check List - Filter, pumps, temperature, testing water level, pH, chlorine, clean & check skimmer/ baskets, brush sides, leaf skimming, vacuum pool, stock of chemicals, first aid supplies, check fences & gates, overall water clarity
2. Items Purchased
3. Items Needed To Purchase
4. Notes & Further Observations Sections
5. Daily Inspection Record
6. Bi-Hourly Water Tests

POOL MAINTENANCE CHECKLIST

DATE		NUMBER OF DAYS SINCE LAST CHECK	

CHECK LIST	CHECKED?	NOTES / COMMENTS
CHECK FILTERS	○ YES ○ NO	
CHECK PUMPS	○ YES ○ NO	
CHECK WATER TEMPERATURE	○ YES ○ NO	WATER TEMPERATURE:
CHECK WATER LEVEL	○ YES ○ NO	AMOUNT OF WATER ADDED:
WATER TEST PH (IDEAL 7.4 - 7.6)	○ YES ○ NO	PH LEVEL:
WATER TEST CHLORINE (IDEAL 1.5 - 2.5)	○ YES ○ NO	CHLORINE LEVEL: HOW MUCH CHLORINE ADDED, IF APPLICABLE:
CLEAN AND CHECK SKIMMER BASKETS	○ YES ○ NO	
BRUSH SIDES	○ YES ○ NO	
LEAF SKIMMING	○ YES ○ NO	
VACUUM POOL	○ YES ○ NO	
CHECK YOUR STOCK OF POOL CHEMICALS	○ YES ○ NO	CHEMICALS / ITEMS PURCHASED:
CHECK YOUR FIRST AID SUPPLIES	○ YES ○ NO	ITEMS TO PURCHASE:
CHECK POOL SIDE ANY FENCES OR GATES	○ YES ○ NO	IF APPLICABLE, LIST MAINTENANCE REQUIRED:
OVERALL WATER CLARITY		

FUTHER NOTES / OBSERVATIONS

POOL DAILY INSPECTION RECORD

	SAT. / UNSAT.	TIME AM / PM	OPERATOR'S SIGNATURE		SAT. / UNSAT.	TIME AM / PM	OPERATOR'S SIGNATURE
EMERGENCY TELEPHONE 1/2 HOUR BEFORE OPENING				SPINEBOARD			
GROUND FAULT INTER-RUPTER 1/2 HOUR BEFORE OPENING				FIRST AID KIT			
NON-CONDUCTING REACH-ING POLE				2 HEALTH WARNING SIGNS			
2 BUOYANT THROWING AIDS WITH ADEQUATE ROPE				UNSUPERVISED SIGN IF APPLICABLE			

POOL BI-HOURLY WATER TESTS

	1/2 HR BEFORE OPENING	TIME	TIME	TIME	TIME	TIME	TIME	TIME	TIME	TIME	TIME	TIME
	AM / PM	AM /PM	AM/PM	AM/PM	AM/PM	AM/PM	AM/PM	AM/PM	AM/PM	AM/PM	AM/PM	AM/PM
FREE AVAILABLE CHLORINE (F.A.C)												
TOTAL CHLORINE (T.C) / BROMINE												
COMBINE CHLORINE (T.C. - F.C.)												
PH (7.2 - 7.8)												
# OF BATHERS												
WATER CLARITY BLACK DISC VISIBLE FROM 9 METERS												
ALKALINITY MINIMUM 80 MG/L (1X / DAY)												
OPERATORS INITIALS												

RECORS OF ANY EMERGENCY, RESCUE EQUIPMENT BREAKDOWN, BACK WASHING, CHEMICALS ADDED MANUALLY, CLEANING, ETC.	O.R.P. READINGS 12 HOUR BEFORE OPENING + 1X DURING THE DATE	
	WATER METER READINGS	
	MAKEUP WATER ADDED 20 L PER BATHER PER DAY	

POOL MAINTENANCE CHECKLIST

DATE		NUMBER OF DAYS SINCE LAST CHECK	

CHECK LIST	CHECKED?	NOTES / COMMENTS
CHECK FILTERS	○ YES ○ NO	
CHECK PUMPS	○ YES ○ NO	
CHECK WATER TEMPERATURE	○ YES ○ NO	WATER TEMPERATURE:
CHECK WATER LEVEL	○ YES ○ NO	AMOUNT OF WATER ADDED:
WATER TEST PH (IDEAL 7.4 - 7.6)	○ YES ○ NO	PH LEVEL:
WATER TEST CHLORINE (IDEAL 1.5 - 2.5)	○ YES ○ NO	CHLORINE LEVEL: HOW MUCH CHLORINE ADDED, IF APPLICABLE:
CLEAN AND CHECK SKIMMER BASKETS	○ YES ○ NO	
BRUSH SIDES	○ YES ○ NO	
LEAF SKIMMING	○ YES ○ NO	
VACUUM POOL	○ YES ○ NO	
CHECK YOUR STOCK OF POOL CHEMICALS	○ YES ○ NO	CHEMICALS / ITEMS PURCHASED:
CHECK YOUR FIRST AID SUPPLIES	○ YES ○ NO	ITEMS TO PURCHASE:
CHECK POOL SIDE ANY FENCES OR GATES	○ YES ○ NO	IF APPLICABLE, LIST MAINTENANCE REQUIRED:
OVERALL WATER CLARITY		

FUTHER NOTES / OBSERVATIONS

POOL DAILY INSPECTION RECORD

	SAT. / UNSAT.	TIME AM / PM	OPERATOR'S SIGNATURE		SAT. / UNSAT.	TIME AM / PM	OPERATOR'S SIGNATURE
EMERGENCY TELEPHONE 1/2 HOUR BEFORE OPENING				SPINEBOARD			
GROUND FAULT INTERRUPTER 1/2 HOUR BEFORE OPENING				FIRST AID KIT			
NON-CONDUCTING REACHING POLE				2 HEALTH WARNING SIGNS			
2 BUOYANT THROWING AIDS WITH ADEQUATE ROPE				UNSUPERVISED SIGN IF APPLICABLE			

POOL BI-HOURLY WATER TESTS

	1/2 HR BEFORE OPENING	TIME	TIME	TIME	TIME	TIME	TIME	TIME	TIME	TIME	TIME	TIME
	AM / PM	AM/PM	AM/PM	AM/PM	AM/PM	AM/PM	AM/PM	AM/PM	AM/PM	AM/PM	AM/PM	AM/PM
FREE AVAILABLE CHLORINE (F.A.C)												
TOTAL CHLORINE (T.C) / BROMINE												
COMBINE CHLORINE (T.C. - F.C.)												
PH (7.2 - 7.8)												
# OF BATHERS												
WATER CLARITY BLACK DISC VISIBLE FROM 9 METERS												
ALKALINITY MINIMUM 80 MG/L (1X / DAY)												
OPERATORS INITIALS												

RECORS OF ANY EMERGENCY, RESCUE EQUIPMENT BREAKDOWN, BACK WASHING, CHEMICALS ADDED MANUALLY, CLEANING, ETC.	O.R.P. READINGS 12 HOUR BEFORE OPENING + 1X DURING THE DATE	
	WATER METER READINGS	
	MAKEUP WATER ADDED 20 L PER BATHER PER DAY	

POOL MAINTENANCE CHECKLIST

DATE		NUMBER OF DAYS SINCE LAST CHECK	

CHECK LIST	CHECKED?	NOTES / COMMENTS
CHECK FILTERS	○ YES ○ NO	
CHECK PUMPS	○ YES ○ NO	
CHECK WATER TEMPERATURE	○ YES ○ NO	WATER TEMPERATURE:
CHECK WATER LEVEL	○ YES ○ NO	AMOUNT OF WATER ADDED:
WATER TEST PH (IDEAL 7.4 - 7.6)	○ YES ○ NO	PH LEVEL:
WATER TEST CHLORINE (IDEAL 1.5 - 2.5)	○ YES ○ NO	CHLORINE LEVEL: HOW MUCH CHLORINE ADDED, IF APPLICABLE:
CLEAN AND CHECK SKIMMER BASKETS	○ YES ○ NO	
BRUSH SIDES	○ YES ○ NO	
LEAF SKIMMING	○ YES ○ NO	
VACUUM POOL	○ YES ○ NO	
CHECK YOUR STOCK OF POOL CHEMICALS	○ YES ○ NO	CHEMICALS / ITEMS PURCHASED:
CHECK YOUR FIRST AID SUPPLIES	○ YES ○ NO	ITEMS TO PURCHASE:
CHECK POOL SIDE ANY FENCES OR GATES	○ YES ○ NO	IF APPLICABLE, LIST MAINTENANCE REQUIRED:
OVERALL WATER CLARITY		

FUTHER NOTES / OBSERVATIONS

POOL DAILY INSPECTION RECORD

	SAT. / UNSAT.	TIME AM / PM	OPERATOR'S SIGNATURE		SAT. / UNSAT.	TIME AM / PM	OPERATOR'S SIGNATURE
EMERGENCY TELEPHONE 1/2 HOUR BEFORE OPENING				SPINEBOARD			
GROUND FAULT INTERRUPTER 1/2 HOUR BEFORE OPENING				FIRST AID KIT			
NON-CONDUCTING REACHING POLE				2 HEALTH WARNING SIGNS			
2 BUOYANT THROWING AIDS WITH ADEQUATE ROPE				UNSUPERVISED SIGN IF APPLICABLE			

POOL BI-HOURLY WATER TESTS

	1/2 HR BEFORE OPENING	TIME	TIME	TIME	TIME	TIME	TIME	TIME	TIME	TIME	TIME	TIME
	AM / PM	AM/PM	AM/PM	AM/PM	AM/PM	AM/PM	AM/PM	AM/PM	AM/PM	AM/PM	AM/PM	AM/PM
FREE AVAILABLE CHLORINE (F.A.C)												
TOTAL CHLORINE (T.C) / BROMINE												
COMBINE CHLORINE (T.C. - F.C.)												
PH (7.2 - 7.8)												
# OF BATHERS												
WATER CLARITY BLACK DISC VISIBLE FROM 9 METERS												
ALKALINITY MINIMUM 80 MG/L (1X / DAY)												
OPERATORS INITIALS												

RECORS OF ANY EMERGENCY, RESCUE EQUIPMENT BREAKDOWN, BACK WASHING, CHEMICALS ADDED MANUALLY, CLEANING, ETC.	O.R.P. READINGS 12 HOUR BEFORE OPENING + 1X DURING THE DATE	
	WATER METER READINGS	
	MAKEUP WATER ADDED 20 L PER BATHER PER DAY	

POOL MAINTENANCE CHECKLIST

DATE		NUMBER OF DAYS SINCE LAST CHECK	

CHECK LIST	CHECKED?	NOTES / COMMENTS
CHECK FILTERS	○ YES ○ NO	
CHECK PUMPS	○ YES ○ NO	
CHECK WATER TEMPERATURE	○ YES ○ NO	WATER TEMPERATURE:
CHECK WATER LEVEL	○ YES ○ NO	AMOUNT OF WATER ADDED:
WATER TEST PH (IDEAL 7.4 - 7.6)	○ YES ○ NO	PH LEVEL:
WATER TEST CHLORINE (IDEAL 1.5 - 2.5)	○ YES ○ NO	CHLORINE LEVEL: HOW MUCH CHLORINE ADDED, IF APPLICABLE:
CLEAN AND CHECK SKIMMER BASKETS	○ YES ○ NO	
BRUSH SIDES	○ YES ○ NO	
LEAF SKIMMING	○ YES ○ NO	
VACUUM POOL	○ YES ○ NO	
CHECK YOUR STOCK OF POOL CHEMICALS	○ YES ○ NO	CHEMICALS / ITEMS PURCHASED:
CHECK YOUR FIRST AID SUPPLIES	○ YES ○ NO	ITEMS TO PURCHASE:
CHECK POOL SIDE ANY FENCES OR GATES	○ YES ○ NO	IF APPLICABLE, LIST MAINTENANCE REQUIRED:
OVERALL WATER CLARITY		

FUTHER NOTES / OBSERVATIONS

POOL DAILY INSPECTION RECORD

	SAT. / UNSAT.	TIME AM / PM	OPERATOR'S SIGNATURE		SAT. / UNSAT.	TIME AM / PM	OPERATOR'S SIGNATURE
EMERGENCY TELEPHONE 1/2 HOUR BEFORE OPENING				SPINEBOARD			
GROUND FAULT INTER-RUPTER 1/2 HOUR BEFORE OPENING				FIRST AID KIT			
NON-CONDUCTING REACH-ING POLE				2 HEALTH WARNING SIGNS			
2 BUOYANT THROWING AIDS WITH ADEQUATE ROPE				UNSUPERVISED SIGN IF APPLICABLE			

POOL BI-HOURLY WATER TESTS

	1/2 HR BEFORE OPENING AM / PM	TIME AM/PM	TIME AM/PM	TIME AM/PM	TIME AM/PM	TIME AM/PM	TIME AM/PM	TIME AM/PM	TIME AM/PM	TIME AM/PM	TIME AM/PM	TIME AM/PM
FREE AVAILABLE CHLORINE (F.A.C)												
TOTAL CHLORINE (T.C) / BROMINE												
COMBINE CHLORINE (T.C. - F.C.)												
PH (7.2 - 7.8)												
# OF BATHERS												
WATER CLARITY BLACK DISC VISIBLE FROM 9 METERS												
ALKALINITY MINIMUM 80 MG/L (1X / DAY)												
OPERATORS INITIALS												

RECORS OF ANY EMERGENCY, RESCUE EQUIPMENT BREAKDOWN, BACK WASHING, CHEMICALS ADDED MANUALLY, CLEANING, ETC.	O.R.P. READINGS 12 HOUR BEFORE OPENING + 1X DURING THE DATE
	WATER METER READINGS
	MAKEUP WATER ADDED 20 L PER BATHER PER DAY

POOL MAINTENANCE CHECKLIST

DATE		NUMBER OF DAYS SINCE LAST CHECK	

CHECK LIST	CHECKED?	NOTES / COMMENTS
CHECK FILTERS	○ YES　○ NO	
CHECK PUMPS	○ YES　○ NO	
CHECK WATER TEMPERATURE	○ YES　○ NO	WATER TEMPERATURE:
CHECK WATER LEVEL	○ YES　○ NO	AMOUNT OF WATER ADDED:
WATER TEST PH (IDEAL 7.4 - 7.6)	○ YES　○ NO	PH LEVEL:
WATER TEST CHLORINE (IDEAL 1.5 - 2.5)	○ YES　○ NO	CHLORINE LEVEL: HOW MUCH CHLORINE ADDED, IF APPLICABLE:
CLEAN AND CHECK SKIMMER BASKETS	○ YES　○ NO	
BRUSH SIDES	○ YES　○ NO	
LEAF SKIMMING	○ YES　○ NO	
VACUUM POOL	○ YES　○ NO	
CHECK YOUR STOCK OF POOL CHEMICALS	○ YES　○ NO	CHEMICALS / ITEMS PURCHASED:
CHECK YOUR FIRST AID SUPPLIES	○ YES　○ NO	ITEMS TO PURCHASE:
CHECK POOL SIDE ANY FENCES OR GATES	○ YES　○ NO	IF APPLICABLE, LIST MAINTENANCE REQUIRED:
OVERALL WATER CLARITY		

FUTHER NOTES / OBSERVATIONS

POOL DAILY INSPECTION RECORD

	SAT. / UNSAT.	TIME AM / PM	OPERATOR'S SIGNATURE		SAT. / UNSAT.	TIME AM / PM	OPERATOR'S SIGNATURE
EMERGENCY TELEPHONE 1/2 HOUR BEFORE OPENING				SPINEBOARD			
GROUND FAULT INTER-RUPTER 1/2 HOUR BEFORE OPENING				FIRST AID KIT			
NON-CONDUCTING REACHING POLE				2 HEALTH WARNING SIGNS			
2 BUOYANT THROWING AIDS WITH ADEQUATE ROPE				UNSUPERVISED SIGN IF APPLICABLE			

POOL BI-HOURLY WATER TESTS

	1/2 HR BEFORE OPENING	TIME	TIME	TIME	TIME	TIME	TIME	TIME	TIME	TIME	TIME	TIME
	AM / PM	AM/PM	AM/PM	AM/PM	AM/PM	AM/PM	AM/PM	AM/PM	AM/PM	AM/PM	AM/PM	AM/PM
FREE AVAILABLE CHLORINE (F.A.C)												
TOTAL CHLORINE (T.C) / BROMINE												
COMBINE CHLORINE (T.C. - F.C.)												
PH (7.2 - 7.8)												
# OF BATHERS												
WATER CLARITY BLACK DISC VISIBLE FROM 9 METERS												
ALKALINITY MINIMUM 80 MG/L (1X / DAY)												
OPERATORS INITIALS												

RECORS OF ANY EMERGENCY, RESCUE EQUIPMENT BREAKDOWN, BACK WASHING, CHEMICALS ADDED MANUALLY, CLEANING, ETC.	O.R.P. READINGS 12 HOUR BEFORE OPENING + 1X DURING THE DATE	
	WATER METER READINGS	
	MAKEUP WATER ADDED 20 L PER BATHER PER DAY	

POOL MAINTENANCE CHECKLIST

DATE		NUMBER OF DAYS SINCE LAST CHECK	

CHECK LIST	CHECKED?	NOTES / COMMENTS
CHECK FILTERS	○ YES ○ NO	
CHECK PUMPS	○ YES ○ NO	
CHECK WATER TEMPERATURE	○ YES ○ NO	WATER TEMPERATURE:
CHECK WATER LEVEL	○ YES ○ NO	AMOUNT OF WATER ADDED:
WATER TEST PH (IDEAL 7.4 - 7.6)	○ YES ○ NO	PH LEVEL:
WATER TEST CHLORINE (IDEAL 1.5 - 2.5)	○ YES ○ NO	CHLORINE LEVEL: HOW MUCH CHLORINE ADDED, IF APPLICABLE:
CLEAN AND CHECK SKIMMER BASKETS	○ YES ○ NO	
BRUSH SIDES	○ YES ○ NO	
LEAF SKIMMING	○ YES ○ NO	
VACUUM POOL	○ YES ○ NO	
CHECK YOUR STOCK OF POOL CHEMICALS	○ YES ○ NO	CHEMICALS / ITEMS PURCHASED:
CHECK YOUR FIRST AID SUPPLIES	○ YES ○ NO	ITEMS TO PURCHASE:
CHECK POOL SIDE ANY FENCES OR GATES	○ YES ○ NO	IF APPLICABLE, LIST MAINTENANCE REQUIRED:
OVERALL WATER CLARITY		

FUTHER NOTES / OBSERVATIONS

POOL DAILY INSPECTION RECORD

	SAT. / UNSAT.	TIME AM / PM	OPERATOR'S SIGNATURE		SAT. / UNSAT.	TIME AM / PM	OPERATOR'S SIGNATURE
EMERGENCY TELEPHONE 1/2 HOUR BEFORE OPENING				SPINEBOARD			
GROUND FAULT INTERRUPTER 1/2 HOUR BEFORE OPENING				FIRST AID KIT			
NON-CONDUCTING REACHING POLE				2 HEALTH WARNING SIGNS			
2 BUOYANT THROWING AIDS WITH ADEQUATE ROPE				UNSUPERVISED SIGN IF APPLICABLE			

POOL BI-HOURLY WATER TESTS

	1/2 HR BEFORE OPENING	TIME	TIME	TIME	TIME	TIME	TIME	TIME	TIME	TIME	TIME	TIME
	AM / PM	AM/PM	AM/PM	AM/PM	AM/PM	AM/PM	AM/PM	AM/PM	AM/PM	AM/PM	AM/PM	AM/PM
FREE AVAILABLE CHLORINE (F.A.C)												
TOTAL CHLORINE (T.C) / BROMINE												
COMBINE CHLORINE (T.C. - F.C.)												
PH (7.2 - 7.8)												
# OF BATHERS												
WATER CLARITY BLACK DISC VISIBLE FROM 9 METERS												
ALKALINITY MINIMUM 80 MG/L (1X / DAY)												
OPERATORS INITIALS												

RECORS OF ANY EMERGENCY, RESCUE EQUIPMENT BREAKDOWN, BACK WASHING, CHEMICALS ADDED MANUALLY, CLEANING, ETC.	O.R.P. READINGS 12 HOUR BEFORE OPENING + 1X DURING THE DATE
	WATER METER READINGS
	MAKEUP WATER ADDED 20 L PER BATHER PER DAY

POOL MAINTENANCE CHECKLIST

DATE		NUMBER OF DAYS SINCE LAST CHECK	

CHECK LIST	CHECKED?	NOTES / COMMENTS
CHECK FILTERS	○ YES ○ NO	
CHECK PUMPS	○ YES ○ NO	
CHECK WATER TEMPERATURE	○ YES ○ NO	WATER TEMPERATURE:
CHECK WATER LEVEL	○ YES ○ NO	AMOUNT OF WATER ADDED:
WATER TEST PH (IDEAL 7.4 - 7.6)	○ YES ○ NO	PH LEVEL:
WATER TEST CHLORINE (IDEAL 1.5 - 2.5)	○ YES ○ NO	CHLORINE LEVEL: HOW MUCH CHLORINE ADDED, IF APPLICABLE:
CLEAN AND CHECK SKIMMER BASKETS	○ YES ○ NO	
BRUSH SIDES	○ YES ○ NO	
LEAF SKIMMING	○ YES ○ NO	
VACUUM POOL	○ YES ○ NO	
CHECK YOUR STOCK OF POOL CHEMICALS	○ YES ○ NO	CHEMICALS / ITEMS PURCHASED:
CHECK YOUR FIRST AID SUPPLIES	○ YES ○ NO	ITEMS TO PURCHASE:
CHECK POOL SIDE ANY FENCES OR GATES	○ YES ○ NO	IF APPLICABLE, LIST MAINTENANCE REQUIRED:
OVERALL WATER CLARITY		

FUTHER NOTES / OBSERVATIONS

POOL DAILY INSPECTION RECORD

	SAT. / UNSAT.	TIME AM / PM	OPERATOR'S SIGNATURE		SAT. / UNSAT.	TIME AM / PM	OPERATOR'S SIGNATURE
EMERGENCY TELEPHONE 1/2 HOUR BEFORE OPENING				SPINEBOARD			
GROUND FAULT INTER-RUPTER 1/2 HOUR BEFORE OPENING				FIRST AID KIT			
NON-CONDUCTING REACHING POLE				2 HEALTH WARNING SIGNS			
2 BUOYANT THROWING AIDS WITH ADEQUATE ROPE				UNSUPERVISED SIGN IF APPLICABLE			

POOL BI-HOURLY WATER TESTS

	1/2 HR BEFORE OPENING	TIME	TIME	TIME	TIME	TIME	TIME	TIME	TIME	TIME	TIME	TIME
	AM / PM	AM/PM	AM/PM	AM/PM	AM/PM	AM/PM	AM/PM	AM/PM	AM/PM	AM/PM	AM/PM	AM/PM
FREE AVAILABLE CHLORINE (F.A.C)												
TOTAL CHLORINE (T.C) / BROMINE												
COMBINE CHLORINE (T.C. - F.C.)												
PH (7.2 - 7.8)												
# OF BATHERS												
WATER CLARITY BLACK DISC VISIBLE FROM 9 METERS												
ALKALINITY MINIMUM 80 MG/L (1X / DAY)												
OPERATORS INITIALS												

RECORS OF ANY EMERGENCY, RESCUE EQUIPMENT BREAKDOWN, BACK WASHING, CHEMICALS ADDED MANUALLY, CLEANING, ETC.	O.R.P. READINGS 12 HOUR BEFORE OPENING + 1X DURING THE DATE	
	WATER METER READINGS	
	MAKEUP WATER ADDED 20 L PER BATHER PER DAY	

POOL MAINTENANCE CHECKLIST

DATE		NUMBER OF DAYS SINCE LAST CHECK	

CHECK LIST	CHECKED?	NOTES / COMMENTS
CHECK FILTERS	○ YES ○ NO	
CHECK PUMPS	○ YES ○ NO	
CHECK WATER TEMPERATURE	○ YES ○ NO	WATER TEMPERATURE:
CHECK WATER LEVEL	○ YES ○ NO	AMOUNT OF WATER ADDED:
WATER TEST PH (IDEAL 7.4 - 7.6)	○ YES ○ NO	PH LEVEL:
WATER TEST CHLORINE (IDEAL 1.5 - 2.5)	○ YES ○ NO	CHLORINE LEVEL: HOW MUCH CHLORINE ADDED, IF APPLICABLE:
CLEAN AND CHECK SKIMMER BASKETS	○ YES ○ NO	
BRUSH SIDES	○ YES ○ NO	
LEAF SKIMMING	○ YES ○ NO	
VACUUM POOL	○ YES ○ NO	
CHECK YOUR STOCK OF POOL CHEMICALS	○ YES ○ NO	CHEMICALS / ITEMS PURCHASED:
CHECK YOUR FIRST AID SUPPLIES	○ YES ○ NO	ITEMS TO PURCHASE:
CHECK POOL SIDE ANY FENCES OR GATES	○ YES ○ NO	IF APPLICABLE, LIST MAINTENANCE REQUIRED:
OVERALL WATER CLARITY		

FUTHER NOTES / OBSERVATIONS

POOL DAILY INSPECTION RECORD

	SAT. / UNSAT.	TIME AM / PM	OPERATOR'S SIGNATURE		SAT. / UNSAT.	TIME AM / PM	OPERATOR'S SIGNATURE
EMERGENCY TELEPHONE 1/2 HOUR BEFORE OPENING				SPINEBOARD			
GROUND FAULT INTER-RUPTER 1/2 HOUR BEFORE OPENING				FIRST AID KIT			
NON-CONDUCTING REACHING POLE				2 HEALTH WARNING SIGNS			
2 BUOYANT THROWING AIDS WITH ADEQUATE ROPE				UNSUPERVISED SIGN IF APPLICABLE			

POOL BI-HOURLY WATER TESTS

	1/2 HR BEFORE OPENING	TIME	TIME	TIME	TIME	TIME	TIME	TIME	TIME	TIME	TIME	TIME
	AM / PM	AM /PM	AM/PM	AM/PM	AM/PM	AM/PM	AM/PM	AM/PM	AM/PM	AM/PM	AM/PM	AM/PM
FREE AVAILABLE CHLORINE (F.A.C)												
TOTAL CHLORINE (T.C) / BROMINE												
COMBINE CHLORINE (T.C. - F.C.)												
PH (7.2 - 7.8)												
# OF BATHERS												
WATER CLARITY BLACK DISC VISIBLE FROM 9 METERS												
ALKALINITY MINIMUM 80 MG/L (1X / DAY)												
OPERATORS INITIALS												

RECORS OF ANY EMERGENCY, RESCUE EQUIPMENT BREAKDOWN, BACK WASHING, CHEMICALS ADDED MANUALLY, CLEANING, ETC.	O.R.P. READINGS 12 HOUR BEFORE OPENING + 1X DURING THE DATE	
	WATER METER READINGS	
	MAKEUP WATER ADDED 20 L PER BATHER PER DAY	

POOL MAINTENANCE CHECKLIST

DATE		NUMBER OF DAYS SINCE LAST CHECK	

CHECK LIST	CHECKED?	NOTES / COMMENTS
CHECK FILTERS	○ YES ○ NO	
CHECK PUMPS	○ YES ○ NO	
CHECK WATER TEMPERATURE	○ YES ○ NO	WATER TEMPERATURE:
CHECK WATER LEVEL	○ YES ○ NO	AMOUNT OF WATER ADDED:
WATER TEST PH (IDEAL 7.4 - 7.6)	○ YES ○ NO	PH LEVEL:
WATER TEST CHLORINE (IDEAL 1.5 - 2.5)	○ YES ○ NO	CHLORINE LEVEL: HOW MUCH CHLORINE ADDED, IF APPLICABLE:
CLEAN AND CHECK SKIMMER BASKETS	○ YES ○ NO	
BRUSH SIDES	○ YES ○ NO	
LEAF SKIMMING	○ YES ○ NO	
VACUUM POOL	○ YES ○ NO	
CHECK YOUR STOCK OF POOL CHEMICALS	○ YES ○ NO	CHEMICALS / ITEMS PURCHASED:
CHECK YOUR FIRST AID SUPPLIES	○ YES ○ NO	ITEMS TO PURCHASE:
CHECK POOL SIDE ANY FENCES OR GATES	○ YES ○ NO	IF APPLICABLE, LIST MAINTENANCE REQUIRED:
OVERALL WATER CLARITY		

FUTHER NOTES / OBSERVATIONS

POOL DAILY INSPECTION RECORD

	SAT. / UNSAT.	TIME AM / PM	OPERATOR'S SIGNATURE		SAT. / UNSAT.	TIME AM / PM	OPERATOR'S SIGNATURE
EMERGENCY TELEPHONE 1/2 HOUR BEFORE OPENING				SPINEBOARD			
GROUND FAULT INTERRUPTER 1/2 HOUR BEFORE OPENING				FIRST AID KIT			
NON-CONDUCTING REACHING POLE				2 HEALTH WARNING SIGNS			
2 BUOYANT THROWING AIDS WITH ADEQUATE ROPE				UNSUPERVISED SIGN IF APPLICABLE			

POOL BI-HOURLY WATER TESTS

	1/2 HR BEFORE OPENING	TIME	TIME	TIME	TIME	TIME	TIME	TIME	TIME	TIME	TIME	TIME
	AM / PM	AM/PM	AM/PM	AM/PM	AM/PM	AM/PM	AM/PM	AM/PM	AM/PM	AM/PM	AM/PM	AM/PM
FREE AVAILABLE CHLORINE (F.A.C)												
TOTAL CHLORINE (T.C) / BROMINE												
COMBINE CHLORINE (T.C. - F.C.)												
PH (7.2 - 7.8)												
# OF BATHERS												
WATER CLARITY BLACK DISC VISIBLE FROM 9 METERS												
ALKALINITY MINIMUM 80 MG/L (1X / DAY)												
OPERATORS INITIALS												

RECORS OF ANY EMERGENCY, RESCUE EQUIPMENT BREAKDOWN, BACK WASHING, CHEMICALS ADDED MANUALLY, CLEANING, ETC.	O.R.P. READINGS 12 HOUR BEFORE OPENING + 1X DURING THE DATE	
	WATER METER READINGS	
	MAKEUP WATER ADDED 20 L PER BATHER PER DAY	

POOL MAINTENANCE CHECKLIST

DATE		NUMBER OF DAYS SINCE LAST CHECK	

CHECK LIST	CHECKED?	NOTES / COMMENTS
CHECK FILTERS	○ YES ○ NO	
CHECK PUMPS	○ YES ○ NO	
CHECK WATER TEMPERATURE	○ YES ○ NO	WATER TEMPERATURE:
CHECK WATER LEVEL	○ YES ○ NO	AMOUNT OF WATER ADDED:
WATER TEST PH (IDEAL 7.4 - 7.6)	○ YES ○ NO	PH LEVEL:
WATER TEST CHLORINE (IDEAL 1.5 - 2.5)	○ YES ○ NO	CHLORINE LEVEL: HOW MUCH CHLORINE ADDED, IF APPLICABLE:
CLEAN AND CHECK SKIMMER BASKETS	○ YES ○ NO	
BRUSH SIDES	○ YES ○ NO	
LEAF SKIMMING	○ YES ○ NO	
VACUUM POOL	○ YES ○ NO	
CHECK YOUR STOCK OF POOL CHEMICALS	○ YES ○ NO	CHEMICALS / ITEMS PURCHASED:
CHECK YOUR FIRST AID SUPPLIES	○ YES ○ NO	ITEMS TO PURCHASE:
CHECK POOL SIDE ANY FENCES OR GATES	○ YES ○ NO	IF APPLICABLE, LIST MAINTENANCE REQUIRED:
OVERALL WATER CLARITY		

FUTHER NOTES / OBSERVATIONS

POOL DAILY INSPECTION RECORD

	SAT. / UNSAT.	TIME AM / PM	OPERATOR'S SIGNATURE		SAT. / UNSAT.	TIME AM / PM	OPERATOR'S SIGNATURE
EMERGENCY TELEPHONE 1/2 HOUR BEFORE OPENING				SPINEBOARD			
GROUND FAULT INTER-RUPTER 1/2 HOUR BEFORE OPENING				FIRST AID KIT			
NON-CONDUCTING REACHING POLE				2 HEALTH WARNING SIGNS			
2 BUOYANT THROWING AIDS WITH ADEQUATE ROPE				UNSUPERVISED SIGN IF APPLICABLE			

POOL BI-HOURLY WATER TESTS

	1/2 HR BEFORE OPENING	TIME	TIME	TIME	TIME	TIME	TIME	TIME	TIME	TIME	TIME	TIME
	AM / PM	AM /PM	AM/PM	AM/PM	AM/PM	AM/PM	AM/PM	AM/PM	AM/PM	AM/PM	AM/PM	AM/PM
FREE AVAILABLE CHLORINE (F.A.C)												
TOTAL CHLORINE (T.C) / BROMINE												
COMBINE CHLORINE (T.C. - F.C.)												
PH (7.2 - 7.8)												
# OF BATHERS												
WATER CLARITY BLACK DISC VISIBLE FROM 9 METERS												
ALKALINITY MINIMUM 80 MG/L (1X / DAY)												
OPERATORS INITIALS												

RECORS OF ANY EMERGENCY, RESCUE EQUIPMENT BREAKDOWN, BACK WASHING, CHEMICALS ADDED MANUALLY, CLEANING, ETC.	O.R.P. READINGS 12 HOUR BEFORE OPENING + 1X DURING THE DATE	
	WATER METER READINGS	
	MAKEUP WATER ADDED 20 L PER BATHER PER DAY	

POOL MAINTENANCE CHECKLIST

DATE		NUMBER OF DAYS SINCE LAST CHECK	

CHECK LIST	CHECKED?	NOTES / COMMENTS
CHECK FILTERS	○ YES ○ NO	
CHECK PUMPS	○ YES ○ NO	
CHECK WATER TEMPERATURE	○ YES ○ NO	WATER TEMPERATURE:
CHECK WATER LEVEL	○ YES ○ NO	AMOUNT OF WATER ADDED:
WATER TEST PH (IDEAL 7.4 - 7.6)	○ YES ○ NO	PH LEVEL:
WATER TEST CHLORINE (IDEAL 1.5 - 2.5)	○ YES ○ NO	CHLORINE LEVEL: HOW MUCH CHLORINE ADDED, IF APPLICABLE:
CLEAN AND CHECK SKIMMER BASKETS	○ YES ○ NO	
BRUSH SIDES	○ YES ○ NO	
LEAF SKIMMING	○ YES ○ NO	
VACUUM POOL	○ YES ○ NO	
CHECK YOUR STOCK OF POOL CHEMICALS	○ YES ○ NO	CHEMICALS / ITEMS PURCHASED:
CHECK YOUR FIRST AID SUPPLIES	○ YES ○ NO	ITEMS TO PURCHASE:
CHECK POOL SIDE ANY FENCES OR GATES	○ YES ○ NO	IF APPLICABLE, LIST MAINTENANCE REQUIRED:
OVERALL WATER CLARITY		

FUTHER NOTES / OBSERVATIONS

POOL DAILY INSPECTION RECORD

	SAT. / UNSAT.	TIME AM / PM	OPERATOR'S SIGNATURE		SAT. / UNSAT.	TIME AM / PM	OPERATOR'S SIGNATURE
EMERGENCY TELEPHONE 1/2 HOUR BEFORE OPENING				SPINEBOARD			
GROUND FAULT INTERRUPTER 1/2 HOUR BEFORE OPENING				FIRST AID KIT			
NON-CONDUCTING REACHING POLE				2 HEALTH WARNING SIGNS			
2 BUOYANT THROWING AIDS WITH ADEQUATE ROPE				UNSUPERVISED SIGN IF APPLICABLE			

POOL BI-HOURLY WATER TESTS

	1/2 HR BEFORE OPENING	TIME	TIME	TIME	TIME	TIME	TIME	TIME	TIME	TIME	TIME	TIME
	AM / PM	AM /PM	AM/PM	AM/PM	AM/PM	AM/PM	AM/PM	AM/PM	AM/PM	AM/PM	AM/PM	AM/PM
FREE AVAILABLE CHLORINE (F.A.C)												
TOTAL CHLORINE (T.C) / BROMINE												
COMBINE CHLORINE (T.C. - F.C.)												
PH (7.2 - 7.8)												
# OF BATHERS												
WATER CLARITY BLACK DISC VISIBLE FROM 9 METERS												
ALKALINITY MINIMUM 80 MG/L (1X / DAY)												
OPERATORS INITIALS												

RECORS OF ANY EMERGENCY, RESCUE EQUIPMENT BREAKDOWN, BACK WASHING, CHEMICALS ADDED MANUALLY, CLEANING, ETC.	O.R.P. READINGS 12 HOUR BEFORE OPENING + 1X DURING THE DATE
	WATER METER READINGS
	MAKEUP WATER ADDED 20 L PER BATHER PER DAY

POOL MAINTENANCE CHECKLIST

DATE		NUMBER OF DAYS SINCE LAST CHECK	

CHECK LIST	CHECKED?	NOTES / COMMENTS
CHECK FILTERS	○ YES ○ NO	
CHECK PUMPS	○ YES ○ NO	
CHECK WATER TEMPERATURE	○ YES ○ NO	WATER TEMPERATURE:
CHECK WATER LEVEL	○ YES ○ NO	AMOUNT OF WATER ADDED:
WATER TEST PH (IDEAL 7.4 - 7.6)	○ YES ○ NO	PH LEVEL:
WATER TEST CHLORINE (IDEAL 1.5 - 2.5)	○ YES ○ NO	CHLORINE LEVEL: HOW MUCH CHLORINE ADDED, IF APPLICABLE:
CLEAN AND CHECK SKIMMER BASKETS	○ YES ○ NO	
BRUSH SIDES	○ YES ○ NO	
LEAF SKIMMING	○ YES ○ NO	
VACUUM POOL	○ YES ○ NO	
CHECK YOUR STOCK OF POOL CHEMICALS	○ YES ○ NO	CHEMICALS / ITEMS PURCHASED:
CHECK YOUR FIRST AID SUPPLIES	○ YES ○ NO	ITEMS TO PURCHASE:
CHECK POOL SIDE ANY FENCES OR GATES	○ YES ○ NO	IF APPLICABLE, LIST MAINTENANCE REQUIRED:
OVERALL WATER CLARITY		

FUTHER NOTES / OBSERVATIONS

POOL DAILY INSPECTION RECORD

	SAT. / UNSAT.	TIME AM / PM	OPERATOR'S SIGNATURE		SAT. / UNSAT.	TIME AM / PM	OPERATOR'S SIGNATURE
EMERGENCY TELEPHONE 1/2 HOUR BEFORE OPENING				SPINEBOARD			
GROUND FAULT INTER-RUPTER 1/2 HOUR BEFORE OPENING				FIRST AID KIT			
NON-CONDUCTING REACHING POLE				2 HEALTH WARNING SIGNS			
2 BUOYANT THROWING AIDS WITH ADEQUATE ROPE				UNSUPERVISED SIGN IF APPLICABLE			

POOL BI-HOURLY WATER TESTS

	1/2 HR BEFORE OPENING	TIME	TIME	TIME	TIME	TIME	TIME	TIME	TIME	TIME	TIME	TIME
	AM / PM	AM/PM	AM/PM	AM/PM	AM/PM	AM/PM	AM/PM	AM/PM	AM/PM	AM/PM	AM/PM	AM/PM
FREE AVAILABLE CHLORINE (F.A.C)												
TOTAL CHLORINE (T.C) / BROMINE												
COMBINE CHLORINE (T.C. - F.C.)												
PH (7.2 - 7.8)												
# OF BATHERS												
WATER CLARITY BLACK DISC VISIBLE FROM 9 METERS												
ALKALINITY MINIMUM 80 MG/L (1X / DAY)												
OPERATORS INITIALS												

RECORS OF ANY EMERGENCY, RESCUE EQUIPMENT BREAKDOWN, BACK WASHING, CHEMICALS ADDED MANUALLY, CLEANING, ETC.	O.R.P. READINGS 12 HOUR BEFORE OPENING + 1X DURING THE DATE	
	WATER METER READINGS	
	MAKEUP WATER ADDED 20 L PER BATHER PER DAY	

POOL MAINTENANCE CHECKLIST

DATE		NUMBER OF DAYS SINCE LAST CHECK	

CHECK LIST	CHECKED?	NOTES / COMMENTS
CHECK FILTERS	○ YES ○ NO	
CHECK PUMPS	○ YES ○ NO	
CHECK WATER TEMPERATURE	○ YES ○ NO	WATER TEMPERATURE:
CHECK WATER LEVEL	○ YES ○ NO	AMOUNT OF WATER ADDED:
WATER TEST PH (IDEAL 7.4 - 7.6)	○ YES ○ NO	PH LEVEL:
WATER TEST CHLORINE (IDEAL 1.5 - 2.5)	○ YES ○ NO	CHLORINE LEVEL: HOW MUCH CHLORINE ADDED, IF APPLICABLE:
CLEAN AND CHECK SKIMMER BASKETS	○ YES ○ NO	
BRUSH SIDES	○ YES ○ NO	
LEAF SKIMMING	○ YES ○ NO	
VACUUM POOL	○ YES ○ NO	
CHECK YOUR STOCK OF POOL CHEMICALS	○ YES ○ NO	CHEMICALS / ITEMS PURCHASED:
CHECK YOUR FIRST AID SUPPLIES	○ YES ○ NO	ITEMS TO PURCHASE:
CHECK POOL SIDE ANY FENCES OR GATES	○ YES ○ NO	IF APPLICABLE, LIST MAINTENANCE REQUIRED:
OVERALL WATER CLARITY		

FUTHER NOTES / OBSERVATIONS

POOL DAILY INSPECTION RECORD

	SAT. / UNSAT.	TIME AM / PM	OPERATOR'S SIGNATURE		SAT. / UNSAT.	TIME AM / PM	OPERATOR'S SIGNATURE
EMERGENCY TELEPHONE 1/2 HOUR BEFORE OPENING				SPINEBOARD			
GROUND FAULT INTER-RUPTER 1/2 HOUR BEFORE OPENING				FIRST AID KIT			
NON-CONDUCTING REACH-ING POLE				2 HEALTH WARNING SIGNS			
2 BUOYANT THROWING AIDS WITH ADEQUATE ROPE				UNSUPERVISED SIGN IF APPLICABLE			

POOL BI-HOURLY WATER TESTS

	1/2 HR BEFORE OPENING	TIME	TIME	TIME	TIME	TIME	TIME	TIME	TIME	TIME	TIME
	AM / PM	AM/PM	AM/PM	AM/PM	AM/PM	AM/PM	AM/PM	AM/PM	AM/PM	AM/PM	AM/PM
FREE AVAILABLE CHLORINE (F.A.C)											
TOTAL CHLORINE (T.C) / BROMINE											
COMBINE CHLORINE (T.C. - F.C.)											
PH (7.2 - 7.8)											
# OF BATHERS											
WATER CLARITY BLACK DISC VISIBLE FROM 9 METERS											
ALKALINITY MINIMUM 80 MG/L. (1X / DAY)											
OPERATORS INITIALS											

RECORS OF ANY EMERGENCY, RESCUE EQUIPMENT BREAKDOWN, BACK WASHING, CHEMICALS ADDED MANUALLY, CLEANING, ETC.	O.R.P. READINGS 12 HOUR BEFORE OPENING + 1X DURING THE DATE	
	WATER METER READINGS	
	MAKEUP WATER ADDED 20 L PER BATHER PER DAY	

POOL MAINTENANCE CHECKLIST

DATE		NUMBER OF DAYS SINCE LAST CHECK	

CHECK LIST	CHECKED?	NOTES / COMMENTS
CHECK FILTERS	○ YES ○ NO	
CHECK PUMPS	○ YES ○ NO	
CHECK WATER TEMPERATURE	○ YES ○ NO	WATER TEMPERATURE:
CHECK WATER LEVEL	○ YES ○ NO	AMOUNT OF WATER ADDED:
WATER TEST PH (IDEAL 7.4 - 7.6)	○ YES ○ NO	PH LEVEL:
WATER TEST CHLORINE (IDEAL 1.5 - 2.5)	○ YES ○ NO	CHLORINE LEVEL: HOW MUCH CHLORINE ADDED, IF APPLICABLE:
CLEAN AND CHECK SKIMMER BASKETS	○ YES ○ NO	
BRUSH SIDES	○ YES ○ NO	
LEAF SKIMMING	○ YES ○ NO	
VACUUM POOL	○ YES ○ NO	
CHECK YOUR STOCK OF POOL CHEMICALS	○ YES ○ NO	CHEMICALS / ITEMS PURCHASED:
CHECK YOUR FIRST AID SUPPLIES	○ YES ○ NO	ITEMS TO PURCHASE:
CHECK POOL SIDE ANY FENCES OR GATES	○ YES ○ NO	IF APPLICABLE, LIST MAINTENANCE REQUIRED:
OVERALL WATER CLARITY		

FUTHER NOTES / OBSERVATIONS

POOL DAILY INSPECTION RECORD

	SAT. / UNSAT.	TIME AM / PM	OPERATOR'S SIGNATURE		SAT. / UNSAT.	TIME AM / PM	OPERATOR'S SIGNATURE
EMERGENCY TELEPHONE 1/2 HOUR BEFORE OPENING				SPINEBOARD			
GROUND FAULT INTERRUPTER 1/2 HOUR BEFORE OPENING				FIRST AID KIT			
NON-CONDUCTING REACHING POLE				2 HEALTH WARNING SIGNS			
2 BUOYANT THROWING AIDS WITH ADEQUATE ROPE				UNSUPERVISED SIGN IF APPLICABLE			

POOL BI-HOURLY WATER TESTS

	1/2 HR BEFORE OPENING	TIME	TIME	TIME	TIME	TIME	TIME	TIME	TIME	TIME	TIME	TIME
	AM / PM	AM /PM	AM/PM	AM/PM	AM/PM	AM/PM	AM/PM	AM/PM	AM/PM	AM/PM	AM/PM	AM/PM
FREE AVAILABLE CHLORINE (F.A.C)												
TOTAL CHLORINE (T.C) / BROMINE												
COMBINE CHLORINE (T.C. - F.C.)												
PH (7.2 - 7.8)												
# OF BATHERS												
WATER CLARITY BLACK DISC VISIBLE FROM 9 METERS												
ALKALINITY MINIMUM 80 MG/L (1X / DAY)												
OPERATORS INITIALS												

RECORS OF ANY EMERGENCY, RESCUE EQUIPMENT BREAKDOWN, BACK WASHING, CHEMICALS ADDED MANUALLY, CLEANING, ETC.	O.R.P. READINGS 12 HOUR BEFORE OPENING + 1X DURING THE DATE	
	WATER METER READINGS	
	MAKEUP WATER ADDED 20 L PER BATHER PER DAY	

POOL MAINTENANCE CHECKLIST

DATE		NUMBER OF DAYS SINCE LAST CHECK	

CHECK LIST	CHECKED?	NOTES / COMMENTS
CHECK FILTERS	○ YES ○ NO	
CHECK PUMPS	○ YES ○ NO	
CHECK WATER TEMPERATURE	○ YES ○ NO	WATER TEMPERATURE:
CHECK WATER LEVEL	○ YES ○ NO	AMOUNT OF WATER ADDED:
WATER TEST PH (IDEAL 7.4 - 7.6)	○ YES ○ NO	PH LEVEL:
WATER TEST CHLORINE (IDEAL 1.5 - 2.5)	○ YES ○ NO	CHLORINE LEVEL: HOW MUCH CHLORINE ADDED, IF APPLICABLE:
CLEAN AND CHECK SKIMMER BASKETS	○ YES ○ NO	
BRUSH SIDES	○ YES ○ NO	
LEAF SKIMMING	○ YES ○ NO	
VACUUM POOL	○ YES ○ NO	
CHECK YOUR STOCK OF POOL CHEMICALS	○ YES ○ NO	CHEMICALS / ITEMS PURCHASED:
CHECK YOUR FIRST AID SUPPLIES	○ YES ○ NO	ITEMS TO PURCHASE:
CHECK POOL SIDE ANY FENCES OR GATES	○ YES ○ NO	IF APPLICABLE, LIST MAINTENANCE REQUIRED:
OVERALL WATER CLARITY		

FUTHER NOTES / OBSERVATIONS

POOL DAILY INSPECTION RECORD

	SAT. / UNSAT.	TIME AM / PM	OPERATOR'S SIGNATURE		SAT. / UNSAT.	TIME AM / PM	OPERATOR'S SIGNATURE
EMERGENCY TELEPHONE 1/2 HOUR BEFORE OPENING				**SPINEBOARD**			
GROUND FAULT INTERRUPTER 1/2 HOUR BEFORE OPENING				**FIRST AID KIT**			
NON-CONDUCTING REACHING POLE				**2 HEALTH WARNING SIGNS**			
2 BUOYANT THROWING AIDS WITH ADEQUATE ROPE				**UNSUPERVISED SIGN** IF APPLICABLE			

POOL BI-HOURLY WATER TESTS

	1/2 HR BEFORE OPENING	TIME	TIME	TIME	TIME	TIME	TIME	TIME	TIME	TIME	TIME	TIME
	AM / PM	AM/PM	AM/PM	AM/PM	AM/PM	AM/PM	AM/PM	AM/PM	AM/PM	AM/PM	AM/PM	AM/PM
FREE AVAILABLE CHLORINE (F.A.C)												
TOTAL CHLORINE (T.C) / BROMINE												
COMBINE CHLORINE (T.C. - F.C.)												
PH (7.2 - 7.8)												
# OF BATHERS												
WATER CLARITY BLACK DISC VISIBLE FROM 9 METERS												
ALKALINITY MINIMUM 80 MG/L (1X / DAY)												
OPERATORS INITIALS												

RECORS OF ANY EMERGENCY, RESCUE EQUIPMENT BREAKDOWN, BACK WASHING, CHEMICALS ADDED MANUALLY, CLEANING, ETC.	O.R.P. READINGS 12 HOUR BEFORE OPENING + 1X DURING THE DATE	
	WATER METER READINGS	
	MAKEUP WATER ADDED 20 L PER BATHER PER DAY	

POOL MAINTENANCE CHECKLIST

DATE		NUMBER OF DAYS SINCE LAST CHECK	

CHECK LIST	CHECKED?	NOTES / COMMENTS
CHECK FILTERS	○ YES ○ NO	
CHECK PUMPS	○ YES ○ NO	
CHECK WATER TEMPERATURE	○ YES ○ NO	WATER TEMPERATURE:
CHECK WATER LEVEL	○ YES ○ NO	AMOUNT OF WATER ADDED:
WATER TEST PH (IDEAL 7.4 - 7.6)	○ YES ○ NO	PH LEVEL:
WATER TEST CHLORINE (IDEAL 1.5 - 2.5)	○ YES ○ NO	CHLORINE LEVEL: HOW MUCH CHLORINE ADDED, IF APPLICABLE:
CLEAN AND CHECK SKIMMER BASKETS	○ YES ○ NO	
BRUSH SIDES	○ YES ○ NO	
LEAF SKIMMING	○ YES ○ NO	
VACUUM POOL	○ YES ○ NO	
CHECK YOUR STOCK OF POOL CHEMICALS	○ YES ○ NO	CHEMICALS / ITEMS PURCHASED:
CHECK YOUR FIRST AID SUPPLIES	○ YES ○ NO	ITEMS TO PURCHASE:
CHECK POOL SIDE ANY FENCES OR GATES	○ YES ○ NO	IF APPLICABLE, LIST MAINTENANCE REQUIRED:
OVERALL WATER CLARITY		

FUTHER NOTES / OBSERVATIONS

POOL DAILY INSPECTION RECORD

	SAT. / UNSAT.	TIME AM / PM	OPERATOR'S SIGNATURE		SAT. / UNSAT.	TIME AM / PM	OPERATOR'S SIGNATURE
EMERGENCY TELEPHONE 1/2 HOUR BEFORE OPENING				SPINEBOARD			
GROUND FAULT INTER-RUPTER 1/2 HOUR BEFORE OPENING				FIRST AID KIT			
NON-CONDUCTING REACHING POLE				2 HEALTH WARNING SIGNS			
2 BUOYANT THROWING AIDS WITH ADEQUATE ROPE				UNSUPERVISED SIGN IF APPLICABLE			

POOL BI-HOURLY WATER TESTS

	1/2 HR BEFORE OPENING	TIME	TIME	TIME	TIME	TIME	TIME	TIME	TIME	TIME	TIME
	AM / PM	AM /PM	AM/PM	AM/PM	AM/PM	AM/PM	AM/PM	AM/PM	AM/PM	AM/PM	AM/PM
FREE AVAILABLE CHLORINE (F.A.C)											
TOTAL CHLORINE (T.C) / BROMINE											
COMBINE CHLORINE (T.C. - F.C.)											
PH (7.2 - 7.8)											
# OF BATHERS											
WATER CLARITY BLACK DISC VISIBLE FROM 9 METERS											
ALKALINITY MINIMUM 80 MG/L (1X / DAY)											
OPERATORS INITIALS											

RECORS OF ANY EMERGENCY, RESCUE EQUIPMENT BREAKDOWN, BACK WASHING, CHEMICALS ADDED MANUALLY, CLEANING, ETC.	O.R.P. READINGS 12 HOUR BEFORE OPENING + 1X DURING THE DATE
	WATER METER READINGS
	MAKEUP WATER ADDED 20 L PER BATHER PER DAY

POOL MAINTENANCE CHECKLIST

DATE		NUMBER OF DAYS SINCE LAST CHECK	

CHECK LIST	CHECKED?	NOTES / COMMENTS
CHECK FILTERS	○ YES ○ NO	
CHECK PUMPS	○ YES ○ NO	
CHECK WATER TEMPERATURE	○ YES ○ NO	WATER TEMPERATURE:
CHECK WATER LEVEL	○ YES ○ NO	AMOUNT OF WATER ADDED:
WATER TEST PH (IDEAL 7.4 - 7.6)	○ YES ○ NO	PH LEVEL:
WATER TEST CHLORINE (IDEAL 1.5 - 2.5)	○ YES ○ NO	CHLORINE LEVEL: HOW MUCH CHLORINE ADDED, IF APPLICABLE:
CLEAN AND CHECK SKIMMER BASKETS	○ YES ○ NO	
BRUSH SIDES	○ YES ○ NO	
LEAF SKIMMING	○ YES ○ NO	
VACUUM POOL	○ YES ○ NO	
CHECK YOUR STOCK OF POOL CHEMICALS	○ YES ○ NO	CHEMICALS / ITEMS PURCHASED:
CHECK YOUR FIRST AID SUPPLIES	○ YES ○ NO	ITEMS TO PURCHASE:
CHECK POOL SIDE ANY FENCES OR GATES	○ YES ○ NO	IF APPLICABLE, LIST MAINTENANCE REQUIRED:
OVERALL WATER CLARITY		

FUTHER NOTES / OBSERVATIONS

POOL DAILY INSPECTION RECORD

	SAT. / UNSAT.	TIME AM / PM	OPERATOR'S SIGNATURE		SAT. / UNSAT.	TIME AM / PM	OPERATOR'S SIGNATURE
EMERGENCY TELEPHONE 1/2 HOUR BEFORE OPENING				SPINEBOARD			
GROUND FAULT INTERRUPTER 1/2 HOUR BEFORE OPENING				FIRST AID KIT			
NON-CONDUCTING REACHING POLE				2 HEALTH WARNING SIGNS			
2 BUOYANT THROWING AIDS WITH ADEQUATE ROPE				UNSUPERVISED SIGN IF APPLICABLE			

POOL BI-HOURLY WATER TESTS

	1/2 HR BEFORE OPENING	TIME	TIME	TIME	TIME	TIME	TIME	TIME	TIME	TIME	TIME	TIME
	AM / PM	AM /PM	AM/PM	AM/PM	AM/PM	AM/PM	AM/PM	AM/PM	AM/PM	AM/PM	AM/PM	AM/PM
FREE AVAILABLE CHLORINE (F.A.C)												
TOTAL CHLORINE (T.C) / BROMINE												
COMBINE CHLORINE (T.C. - F.C.)												
PH (7.2 - 7.8)												
# OF BATHERS												
WATER CLARITY BLACK DISC VISIBLE FROM 9 METERS												
ALKALINITY MINIMUM 80 MG/L (1X / DAY)												
OPERATORS INITIALS												

RECORS OF ANY EMERGENCY, RESCUE EQUIPMENT BREAKDOWN, BACK WASHING, CHEMICALS ADDED MANUALLY, CLEANING, ETC.	O.R.P. READINGS 12 HOUR BEFORE OPENING + 1X DURING THE DATE	
	WATER METER READINGS	
	MAKEUP WATER ADDED 20 L PER BATHER PER DAY	

POOL MAINTENANCE CHECKLIST

DATE		NUMBER OF DAYS SINCE LAST CHECK	

CHECK LIST	CHECKED?	NOTES / COMMENTS
CHECK FILTERS	○ YES ○ NO	
CHECK PUMPS	○ YES ○ NO	
CHECK WATER TEMPERATURE	○ YES ○ NO	WATER TEMPERATURE:
CHECK WATER LEVEL	○ YES ○ NO	AMOUNT OF WATER ADDED:
WATER TEST PH (IDEAL 7.4 - 7.6)	○ YES ○ NO	PH LEVEL:
WATER TEST CHLORINE (IDEAL 1.5 - 2.5)	○ YES ○ NO	CHLORINE LEVEL: HOW MUCH CHLORINE ADDED, IF APPLICABLE:
CLEAN AND CHECK SKIMMER BASKETS	○ YES ○ NO	
BRUSH SIDES	○ YES ○ NO	
LEAF SKIMMING	○ YES ○ NO	
VACUUM POOL	○ YES ○ NO	
CHECK YOUR STOCK OF POOL CHEMICALS	○ YES ○ NO	CHEMICALS / ITEMS PURCHASED:
CHECK YOUR FIRST AID SUPPLIES	○ YES ○ NO	ITEMS TO PURCHASE:
CHECK POOL SIDE ANY FENCES OR GATES	○ YES ○ NO	IF APPLICABLE, LIST MAINTENANCE REQUIRED:
OVERALL WATER CLARITY		

FUTHER NOTES / OBSERVATIONS

POOL DAILY INSPECTION RECORD

	SAT. / UNSAT.	TIME AM / PM	OPERATOR'S SIGNATURE		SAT. / UNSAT.	TIME AM / PM	OPERATOR'S SIGNATURE
EMERGENCY TELEPHONE 1/2 HOUR BEFORE OPENING				SPINEBOARD			
GROUND FAULT INTER-RUPTER 1/2 HOUR BEFORE OPENING				FIRST AID KIT			
NON-CONDUCTING REACHING POLE				2 HEALTH WARNING SIGNS			
2 BUOYANT THROWING AIDS WITH ADEQUATE ROPE				UNSUPERVISED SIGN IF APPLICABLE			

POOL BI-HOURLY WATER TESTS

	1/2 HR BEFORE OPENING	TIME	TIME	TIME	TIME	TIME	TIME	TIME	TIME	TIME	TIME	TIME
	AM / PM	AM /PM	AM/PM	AM/PM	AM/PM	AM/PM	AM/PM	AM/PM	AM/PM	AM/PM	AM/PM	AM/PM
FREE AVAILABLE CHLORINE (F.A.C)												
TOTAL CHLORINE (T.C) / BROMINE												
COMBINE CHLORINE (T.C - F.C.)												
PH (7.2 - 7.8)												
# OF BATHERS												
WATER CLARITY BLACK DISC VISIBLE FROM 9 METERS												
ALKALINITY MINIMUM 80 MG/L (1X / DAY)												
OPERATORS INITIALS												

RECORS OF ANY EMERGENCY, RESCUE EQUIPMENT BREAKDOWN, BACK WASHING, CHEMICALS ADDED MANUALLY, CLEANING, ETC.	O.R.P. READINGS 12 HOUR BEFORE OPENING + 1X DURING THE DATE	
	WATER METER READINGS	
	MAKEUP WATER ADDED 20 L PER BATHER PER DAY	

POOL MAINTENANCE CHECKLIST

DATE		NUMBER OF DAYS SINCE LAST CHECK	

CHECK LIST	CHECKED?	NOTES / COMMENTS
CHECK FILTERS	○ YES ○ NO	
CHECK PUMPS	○ YES ○ NO	
CHECK WATER TEMPERATURE	○ YES ○ NO	WATER TEMPERATURE:
CHECK WATER LEVEL	○ YES ○ NO	AMOUNT OF WATER ADDED:
WATER TEST PH (IDEAL 7.4 - 7.6)	○ YES ○ NO	PH LEVEL:
WATER TEST CHLORINE (IDEAL 1.5 - 2.5)	○ YES ○ NO	CHLORINE LEVEL: HOW MUCH CHLORINE ADDED, IF APPLICABLE:
CLEAN AND CHECK SKIMMER BASKETS	○ YES ○ NO	
BRUSH SIDES	○ YES ○ NO	
LEAF SKIMMING	○ YES ○ NO	
VACUUM POOL	○ YES ○ NO	
CHECK YOUR STOCK OF POOL CHEMICALS	○ YES ○ NO	CHEMICALS / ITEMS PURCHASED:
CHECK YOUR FIRST AID SUPPLIES	○ YES ○ NO	ITEMS TO PURCHASE:
CHECK POOL SIDE ANY FENCES OR GATES	○ YES ○ NO	IF APPLICABLE, LIST MAINTENANCE REQUIRED:
OVERALL WATER CLARITY		

FUTHER NOTES / OBSERVATIONS

POOL DAILY INSPECTION RECORD

	SAT. / UNSAT.	TIME AM / PM	OPERATOR'S SIGNATURE		SAT. / UNSAT.	TIME AM / PM	OPERATOR'S SIGNATURE
EMERGENCY TELEPHONE 1/2 HOUR BEFORE OPENING				SPINEBOARD			
GROUND FAULT INTERRUPTER 1/2 HOUR BEFORE OPENING				FIRST AID KIT			
NON-CONDUCTING REACHING POLE				2 HEALTH WARNING SIGNS			
2 BUOYANT THROWING AIDS WITH ADEQUATE ROPE				UNSUPERVISED SIGN IF APPLICABLE			

POOL BI-HOURLY WATER TESTS

	1/2 HR BEFORE OPENING	TIME	TIME	TIME	TIME	TIME	TIME	TIME	TIME	TIME	TIME	TIME
	AM / PM	AM /PM	AM/PM	AM/PM	AM/PM	AM/PM	AM/PM	AM/PM	AM/PM	AM/PM	AM/PM	AM/PM
FREE AVAILABLE CHLORINE (F.A.C)												
TOTAL CHLORINE (T.C) / BROMINE												
COMBINE CHLORINE (T.C. - F.C.)												
PH (7.2 - 7.8)												
# OF BATHERS												
WATER CLARITY BLACK DISC VISIBLE FROM 9 METERS												
ALKALINITY MINIMUM 80 MG/L (1X / DAY)												
OPERATORS INITIALS												

RECORS OF ANY EMERGENCY, RESCUE EQUIPMENT BREAKDOWN, BACK WASHING, CHEMICALS ADDED MANUALLY, CLEANING, ETC.	O.R.P. READINGS 12 HOUR BEFORE OPENING + 1X DURING THE DATE	
	WATER METER READINGS	
	MAKEUP WATER ADDED 20 L PER BATHER PER DAY	

POOL MAINTENANCE CHECKLIST

DATE		NUMBER OF DAYS SINCE LAST CHECK	

CHECK LIST	CHECKED?	NOTES / COMMENTS
CHECK FILTERS	○ YES ○ NO	
CHECK PUMPS	○ YES ○ NO	
CHECK WATER TEMPERATURE	○ YES ○ NO	WATER TEMPERATURE:
CHECK WATER LEVEL	○ YES ○ NO	AMOUNT OF WATER ADDED:
WATER TEST PH (IDEAL 7.4 - 7.6)	○ YES ○ NO	PH LEVEL:
WATER TEST CHLORINE (IDEAL 1.5 - 2.5)	○ YES ○ NO	CHLORINE LEVEL: HOW MUCH CHLORINE ADDED, IF APPLICABLE:
CLEAN AND CHECK SKIMMER BASKETS	○ YES ○ NO	
BRUSH SIDES	○ YES ○ NO	
LEAF SKIMMING	○ YES ○ NO	
VACUUM POOL	○ YES ○ NO	
CHECK YOUR STOCK OF POOL CHEMICALS	○ YES ○ NO	CHEMICALS / ITEMS PURCHASED:
CHECK YOUR FIRST AID SUPPLIES	○ YES ○ NO	ITEMS TO PURCHASE:
CHECK POOL SIDE ANY FENCES OR GATES	○ YES ○ NO	IF APPLICABLE, LIST MAINTENANCE REQUIRED:
OVERALL WATER CLARITY		

FUTHER NOTES / OBSERVATIONS

POOL DAILY INSPECTION RECORD

	SAT. / UNSAT.	TIME AM / PM	OPERATOR'S SIGNATURE		SAT. / UNSAT.	TIME AM / PM	OPERATOR'S SIGNATURE
EMERGENCY TELEPHONE 1/2 HOUR BEFORE OPENING				SPINEBOARD			
GROUND FAULT INTER-RUPTER 1/2 HOUR BEFORE OPENING				FIRST AID KIT			
NON-CONDUCTING REACHING POLE				2 HEALTH WARNING SIGNS			
2 BUOYANT THROWING AIDS WITH ADEQUATE ROPE				UNSUPERVISED SIGN IF APPLICABLE			

POOL BI-HOURLY WATER TESTS

	1/2 HR BEFORE OPENING AM / PM	TIME AM/PM	TIME AM/PM	TIME AM/PM	TIME AM/PM	TIME AM/PM	TIME AM/PM	TIME AM/PM	TIME AM/PM	TIME AM/PM	TIME AM/PM	TIME AM/PM
FREE AVAILABLE CHLORINE (F.A.C)												
TOTAL CHLORINE (T.C) / BROMINE												
COMBINE CHLORINE (T.C. - F.C.)												
PH (7.2 - 7.8)												
# OF BATHERS												
WATER CLARITY BLACK DISC VISIBLE FROM 9 METERS												
ALKALINITY MINIMUM 80 MG/L (1X / DAY)												
OPERATORS INITIALS												

RECORS OF ANY EMERGENCY, RESCUE EQUIPMENT BREAKDOWN, BACK WASHING, CHEMICALS ADDED MANUALLY, CLEANING, ETC.	O.R.P. READINGS 12 HOUR BEFORE OPENING + 1X DURING THE DATE	
	WATER METER READINGS	
	MAKEUP WATER ADDED 20 L PER BATHER PER DAY	

POOL MAINTENANCE CHECKLIST

DATE		NUMBER OF DAYS SINCE LAST CHECK	

CHECK LIST	CHECKED?	NOTES / COMMENTS
CHECK FILTERS	○ YES ○ NO	
CHECK PUMPS	○ YES ○ NO	
CHECK WATER TEMPERATURE	○ YES ○ NO	WATER TEMPERATURE:
CHECK WATER LEVEL	○ YES ○ NO	AMOUNT OF WATER ADDED:
WATER TEST PH (IDEAL 7.4 - 7.6)	○ YES ○ NO	PH LEVEL:
WATER TEST CHLORINE (IDEAL 1.5 - 2.5)	○ YES ○ NO	CHLORINE LEVEL: HOW MUCH CHLORINE ADDED, IF APPLICABLE:
CLEAN AND CHECK SKIMMER BASKETS	○ YES ○ NO	
BRUSH SIDES	○ YES ○ NO	
LEAF SKIMMING	○ YES ○ NO	
VACUUM POOL	○ YES ○ NO	
CHECK YOUR STOCK OF POOL CHEMICALS	○ YES ○ NO	CHEMICALS / ITEMS PURCHASED:
CHECK YOUR FIRST AID SUPPLIES	○ YES ○ NO	ITEMS TO PURCHASE:
CHECK POOL SIDE ANY FENCES OR GATES	○ YES ○ NO	IF APPLICABLE, LIST MAINTENANCE REQUIRED:
OVERALL WATER CLARITY		

FUTHER NOTES / OBSERVATIONS

POOL DAILY INSPECTION RECORD

	SAT. / UNSAT.	TIME AM / PM	OPERATOR'S SIGNATURE		SAT. / UNSAT.	TIME AM / PM	OPERATOR'S SIGNATURE
EMERGENCY TELEPHONE 1/2 HOUR BEFORE OPENING				SPINEBOARD			
GROUND FAULT INTER-RUPTER 1/2 HOUR BEFORE OPENING				FIRST AID KIT			
NON-CONDUCTING REACH-ING POLE				2 HEALTH WARNING SIGNS			
2 BUOYANT THROWING AIDS WITH ADEQUATE ROPE				UNSUPERVISED SIGN IF APPLICABLE			

POOL BI-HOURLY WATER TESTS

	1/2 HR BEFORE OPENING	TIME	TIME	TIME	TIME	TIME	TIME	TIME	TIME	TIME	TIME	TIME
	AM / PM	AM/PM	AM/PM	AM/PM	AM/PM	AM/PM	AM/PM	AM/PM	AM/PM	AM/PM	AM/PM	AM/PM
FREE AVAILABLE CHLORINE (F.A.C)												
TOTAL CHLORINE (T.C) / BROMINE												
COMBINE CHLORINE (T.C - F.C)												
PH (7.2 - 7.8)												
# OF BATHERS												
WATER CLARITY BLACK DISC VISIBLE FROM 9 METERS												
ALKALINITY MINIMUM 80 MG/L (1X / DAY)												
OPERATORS INITIALS												

RECORS OF ANY EMERGENCY, RESCUE EQUIPMENT BREAKDOWN, BACK WASHING, CHEMICALS ADDED MANUALLY, CLEANING, ETC.	O.R.P. READINGS 12 HOUR BEFORE OPENING + 1X DURING THE DATE	
	WATER METER READINGS	
	MAKEUP WATER ADDED 20 L PER BATHER PER DAY	

POOL MAINTENANCE CHECKLIST

DATE		NUMBER OF DAYS SINCE LAST CHECK	

CHECK LIST	CHECKED?	NOTES / COMMENTS
CHECK FILTERS	○ YES ○ NO	
CHECK PUMPS	○ YES ○ NO	
CHECK WATER TEMPERATURE	○ YES ○ NO	WATER TEMPERATURE:
CHECK WATER LEVEL	○ YES ○ NO	AMOUNT OF WATER ADDED:
WATER TEST PH (IDEAL 7.4 - 7.6)	○ YES ○ NO	PH LEVEL:
WATER TEST CHLORINE (IDEAL 1.5 - 2.5)	○ YES ○ NO	CHLORINE LEVEL: HOW MUCH CHLORINE ADDED, IF APPLICABLE:
CLEAN AND CHECK SKIMMER BASKETS	○ YES ○ NO	
BRUSH SIDES	○ YES ○ NO	
LEAF SKIMMING	○ YES ○ NO	
VACUUM POOL	○ YES ○ NO	
CHECK YOUR STOCK OF POOL CHEMICALS	○ YES ○ NO	CHEMICALS / ITEMS PURCHASED:
CHECK YOUR FIRST AID SUPPLIES	○ YES ○ NO	ITEMS TO PURCHASE:
CHECK POOL SIDE ANY FENCES OR GATES	○ YES ○ NO	IF APPLICABLE, LIST MAINTENANCE REQUIRED:
OVERALL WATER CLARITY		

FUTHER NOTES / OBSERVATIONS

POOL DAILY INSPECTION RECORD

	SAT. / UNSAT.	TIME AM / PM	OPERATOR'S SIGNATURE		SAT. / UNSAT.	TIME AM / PM	OPERATOR'S SIGNATURE
EMERGENCY TELEPHONE 1/2 HOUR BEFORE OPENING				**SPINEBOARD**			
GROUND FAULT INTERRUPTER 1/2 HOUR BEFORE OPENING				**FIRST AID KIT**			
NON-CONDUCTING REACHING POLE				**2 HEALTH WARNING SIGNS**			
2 BUOYANT THROWING AIDS WITH ADEQUATE ROPE				**UNSUPERVISED SIGN** IF APPLICABLE			

POOL BI-HOURLY WATER TESTS

	1/2 HR BEFORE OPENING	TIME	TIME	TIME	TIME	TIME	TIME	TIME	TIME	TIME	TIME	TIME
	AM / PM	AM /PM	AM/PM	AM/PM	AM/PM	AM/PM	AM/PM	AM/PM	AM/PM	AM/PM	AM/PM	AM/PM
FREE AVAILABLE CHLORINE (F.A.C)												
TOTAL CHLORINE (T.C) / BROMINE												
COMBINE CHLORINE (T.C. - F.C.)												
PH (7.2 - 7.8)												
# OF BATHERS												
WATER CLARITY BLACK DISC VISIBLE FROM 9 METERS												
ALKALINITY MINIMUM 80 MG/L (1X / DAY)												
OPERATORS INITIALS												

RECORS OF ANY EMERGENCY, RESCUE EQUIPMENT BREAKDOWN, BACK WASHING, CHEMICALS ADDED MANUALLY, CLEANING, ETC.	O.R.P. READINGS 12 HOUR BEFORE OPENING + 1X DURING THE DATE	
	WATER METER READINGS	
	MAKEUP WATER ADDED 20 L PER BATHER PER DAY	

POOL MAINTENANCE CHECKLIST

DATE		NUMBER OF DAYS SINCE LAST CHECK	

CHECK LIST	CHECKED?	NOTES / COMMENTS
CHECK FILTERS	○ YES ○ NO	
CHECK PUMPS	○ YES ○ NO	
CHECK WATER TEMPERATURE	○ YES ○ NO	WATER TEMPERATURE:
CHECK WATER LEVEL	○ YES ○ NO	AMOUNT OF WATER ADDED:
WATER TEST PH (IDEAL 7.4 - 7.6)	○ YES ○ NO	PH LEVEL:
WATER TEST CHLORINE (IDEAL 1.5 - 2.5)	○ YES ○ NO	CHLORINE LEVEL: HOW MUCH CHLORINE ADDED, IF APPLICABLE:
CLEAN AND CHECK SKIMMER BASKETS	○ YES ○ NO	
BRUSH SIDES	○ YES ○ NO	
LEAF SKIMMING	○ YES ○ NO	
VACUUM POOL	○ YES ○ NO	
CHECK YOUR STOCK OF POOL CHEMICALS	○ YES ○ NO	CHEMICALS / ITEMS PURCHASED:
CHECK YOUR FIRST AID SUPPLIES	○ YES ○ NO	ITEMS TO PURCHASE:
CHECK POOL SIDE ANY FENCES OR GATES	○ YES ○ NO	IF APPLICABLE, LIST MAINTENANCE REQUIRED:
OVERALL WATER CLARITY		

FUTHER NOTES / OBSERVATIONS

POOL DAILY INSPECTION RECORD

	SAT. / UNSAT.	TIME AM / PM	OPERATOR'S SIGNATURE		SAT. / UNSAT.	TIME AM / PM	OPERATOR'S SIGNATURE
EMERGENCY TELEPHONE 1/2 HOUR BEFORE OPENING				SPINEBOARD			
GROUND FAULT INTERRUPTER 1/2 HOUR BEFORE OPENING				FIRST AID KIT			
NON-CONDUCTING REACHING POLE				2 HEALTH WARNING SIGNS			
2 BUOYANT THROWING AIDS WITH ADEQUATE ROPE				UNSUPERVISED SIGN IF APPLICABLE			

POOL BI-HOURLY WATER TESTS

	1/2 HR BEFORE OPENING	TIME	TIME	TIME	TIME	TIME	TIME	TIME	TIME	TIME	TIME	TIME
	AM / PM	AM /PM	AM/PM	AM/PM	AM/PM	AM/PM	AM/PM	AM/PM	AM/PM	AM/PM	AM/PM	AM/PM
FREE AVAILABLE CHLORINE (F.A.C)												
TOTAL CHLORINE (T.C) / BROMINE												
COMBINE CHLORINE (T.C - F.C.)												
PH (7.2 - 7.8)												
# OF BATHERS												
WATER CLARITY BLACK DISC VISIBLE FROM 9 METERS												
ALKALINITY MINIMUM 80 MG/L (1X / DAY)												
OPERATORS INITIALS												

RECORS OF ANY EMERGENCY, RESCUE EQUIPMENT BREAKDOWN, BACK WASHING, CHEMICALS ADDED MANUALLY, CLEANING, ETC.	O.R.P. READINGS 12 HOUR BEFORE OPENING + 1X DURING THE DATE	
	WATER METER READINGS	
	MAKEUP WATER ADDED 20 L PER BATHER PER DAY	

POOL MAINTENANCE CHECKLIST

DATE		NUMBER OF DAYS SINCE LAST CHECK	

CHECK LIST	CHECKED?	NOTES / COMMENTS
CHECK FILTERS	○ YES ○ NO	
CHECK PUMPS	○ YES ○ NO	
CHECK WATER TEMPERATURE	○ YES ○ NO	WATER TEMPERATURE:
CHECK WATER LEVEL	○ YES ○ NO	AMOUNT OF WATER ADDED:
WATER TEST PH (IDEAL 7.4 - 7.6)	○ YES ○ NO	PH LEVEL:
WATER TEST CHLORINE (IDEAL 1.5 - 2.5)	○ YES ○ NO	CHLORINE LEVEL: HOW MUCH CHLORINE ADDED, IF APPLICABLE:
CLEAN AND CHECK SKIMMER BASKETS	○ YES ○ NO	
BRUSH SIDES	○ YES ○ NO	
LEAF SKIMMING	○ YES ○ NO	
VACUUM POOL	○ YES ○ NO	
CHECK YOUR STOCK OF POOL CHEMICALS	○ YES ○ NO	CHEMICALS / ITEMS PURCHASED:
CHECK YOUR FIRST AID SUPPLIES	○ YES ○ NO	ITEMS TO PURCHASE:
CHECK POOL SIDE ANY FENCES OR GATES	○ YES ○ NO	IF APPLICABLE, LIST MAINTENANCE REQUIRED:
OVERALL WATER CLARITY		

FUTHER NOTES / OBSERVATIONS

POOL DAILY INSPECTION RECORD

	SAT. / UNSAT.	TIME AM / PM	OPERATOR'S SIGNATURE		SAT. / UNSAT.	TIME AM / PM	OPERATOR'S SIGNATURE
EMERGENCY TELEPHONE 1/2 HOUR BEFORE OPENING				SPINEBOARD			
GROUND FAULT INTERRUPTER 1/2 HOUR BEFORE OPENING				FIRST AID KIT			
NON-CONDUCTING REACHING POLE				2 HEALTH WARNING SIGNS			
2 BUOYANT THROWING AIDS WITH ADEQUATE ROPE				UNSUPERVISED SIGN IF APPLICABLE			

POOL BI-HOURLY WATER TESTS

	1/2 HR BEFORE OPENING	TIME	TIME	TIME	TIME	TIME	TIME	TIME	TIME	TIME	TIME	TIME
	AM / PM	AM/PM	AM/PM	AM/PM	AM/PM	AM/PM	AM/PM	AM/PM	AM/PM	AM/PM	AM/PM	AM/PM
FREE AVAILABLE CHLORINE (F.A.C)												
TOTAL CHLORINE (T.C) / BROMINE												
COMBINE CHLORINE (T.C - F.C.)												
PH (7.2 - 7.8)												
# OF BATHERS												
WATER CLARITY BLACK DISC VISIBLE FROM 9 METERS												
ALKALINITY MINIMUM 80 MG/L (1X / DAY)												
OPERATORS INITIALS												

RECORS OF ANY EMERGENCY, RESCUE EQUIPMENT BREAKDOWN, BACK WASHING, CHEMICALS ADDED MANUALLY, CLEANING, ETC.	O.R.P. READINGS 12 HOUR BEFORE OPENING + 1X DURING THE DATE	
	WATER METER READINGS	
	MAKEUP WATER ADDED 20 L PER BATHER PER DAY	

POOL MAINTENANCE CHECKLIST

DATE		NUMBER OF DAYS SINCE LAST CHECK	

CHECK LIST	CHECKED?	NOTES / COMMENTS
CHECK FILTERS	○ YES ○ NO	
CHECK PUMPS	○ YES ○ NO	
CHECK WATER TEMPERATURE	○ YES ○ NO	WATER TEMPERATURE:
CHECK WATER LEVEL	○ YES ○ NO	AMOUNT OF WATER ADDED:
WATER TEST PH (IDEAL 7.4 - 7.6)	○ YES ○ NO	PH LEVEL:
WATER TEST CHLORINE (IDEAL 1.5 - 2.5)	○ YES ○ NO	CHLORINE LEVEL: HOW MUCH CHLORINE ADDED, IF APPLICABLE:
CLEAN AND CHECK SKIMMER BASKETS	○ YES ○ NO	
BRUSH SIDES	○ YES ○ NO	
LEAF SKIMMING	○ YES ○ NO	
VACUUM POOL	○ YES ○ NO	
CHECK YOUR STOCK OF POOL CHEMICALS	○ YES ○ NO	CHEMICALS / ITEMS PURCHASED:
CHECK YOUR FIRST AID SUPPLIES	○ YES ○ NO	ITEMS TO PURCHASE:
CHECK POOL SIDE ANY FENCES OR GATES	○ YES ○ NO	IF APPLICABLE, LIST MAINTENANCE REQUIRED:
OVERALL WATER CLARITY		

FUTHER NOTES / OBSERVATIONS

POOL DAILY INSPECTION RECORD

	SAT. / UNSAT.	TIME AM / PM	OPERATOR'S SIGNATURE		SAT. / UNSAT.	TIME AM / PM	OPERATOR'S SIGNATURE
EMERGENCY TELEPHONE 1/2 HOUR BEFORE OPENING				SPINEBOARD			
GROUND FAULT INTERRUPTER 1/2 HOUR BEFORE OPENING				FIRST AID KIT			
NON-CONDUCTING REACHING POLE				2 HEALTH WARNING SIGNS			
2 BUOYANT THROWING AIDS WITH ADEQUATE ROPE				UNSUPERVISED SIGN IF APPLICABLE			

POOL BI-HOURLY WATER TESTS

	1/2 HR BEFORE OPENING	TIME	TIME	TIME	TIME	TIME	TIME	TIME	TIME	TIME	TIME	TIME
	AM / PM	AM /PM	AM/PM	AM/PM	AM/PM	AM/PM	AM/PM	AM/PM	AM/PM	AM/PM	AM/PM	AM/PM
FREE AVAILABLE CHLORINE (F.A.C)												
TOTAL CHLORINE (T.C) / BROMINE												
COMBINE CHLORINE (T.C. - F.C.)												
PH (7.2 - 7.8)												
# OF BATHERS												
WATER CLARITY BLACK DISC VISIBLE FROM 9 METERS												
ALKALINITY MINIMUM 80 MG/L (1X / DAY)												
OPERATORS INITIALS												

RECORS OF ANY EMERGENCY, RESCUE EQUIPMENT BREAKDOWN, BACK WASHING, CHEMICALS ADDED MANUALLY, CLEANING, ETC.	O.R.P. READINGS 12 HOUR BEFORE OPENING + 1X DURING THE DATE	
	WATER METER READINGS	
	MAKEUP WATER ADDED 20 L PER BATHER PER DAY	

POOL MAINTENANCE CHECKLIST

DATE		NUMBER OF DAYS SINCE LAST CHECK	

CHECK LIST	CHECKED?	NOTES / COMMENTS
CHECK FILTERS	○ YES ○ NO	
CHECK PUMPS	○ YES ○ NO	
CHECK WATER TEMPERATURE	○ YES ○ NO	WATER TEMPERATURE:
CHECK WATER LEVEL	○ YES ○ NO	AMOUNT OF WATER ADDED:
WATER TEST PH (IDEAL 7.4 - 7.6)	○ YES ○ NO	PH LEVEL:
WATER TEST CHLORINE (IDEAL 1.5 - 2.5)	○ YES ○ NO	CHLORINE LEVEL: HOW MUCH CHLORINE ADDED, IF APPLICABLE:
CLEAN AND CHECK SKIMMER BASKETS	○ YES ○ NO	
BRUSH SIDES	○ YES ○ NO	
LEAF SKIMMING	○ YES ○ NO	
VACUUM POOL	○ YES ○ NO	
CHECK YOUR STOCK OF POOL CHEMICALS	○ YES ○ NO	CHEMICALS / ITEMS PURCHASED:
CHECK YOUR FIRST AID SUPPLIES	○ YES ○ NO	ITEMS TO PURCHASE:
CHECK POOL SIDE ANY FENCES OR GATES	○ YES ○ NO	IF APPLICABLE, LIST MAINTENANCE REQUIRED:
OVERALL WATER CLARITY		

FUTHER NOTES / OBSERVATIONS

POOL DAILY INSPECTION RECORD

	SAT. / UNSAT.	TIME AM / PM	OPERATOR'S SIGNATURE		SAT. / UNSAT.	TIME AM / PM	OPERATOR'S SIGNATURE
EMERGENCY TELEPHONE 1/2 HOUR BEFORE OPENING				SPINEBOARD			
GROUND FAULT INTERRUPTER 1/2 HOUR BEFORE OPENING				FIRST AID KIT			
NON-CONDUCTING REACHING POLE				2 HEALTH WARNING SIGNS			
2 BUOYANT THROWING AIDS WITH ADEQUATE ROPE				UNSUPERVISED SIGN IF APPLICABLE			

POOL BI-HOURLY WATER TESTS

	1/2 HR BEFORE OPENING	TIME	TIME	TIME	TIME	TIME	TIME	TIME	TIME	TIME	TIME	TIME
	AM / PM	AM/PM	AM/PM	AM/PM	AM/PM	AM/PM	AM/PM	AM/PM	AM/PM	AM/PM	AM/PM	AM/PM
FREE AVAILABLE CHLORINE (F.A.C)												
TOTAL CHLORINE (T.C) / BROMINE												
COMBINE CHLORINE (T.C. - F.C.)												
PH (7.2 - 7.8)												
# OF BATHERS												
WATER CLARITY BLACK DISC VISIBLE FROM 9 METERS												
ALKALINITY MINIMUM 80 MG/L (1X / DAY)												
OPERATORS INITIALS												

RECORS OF ANY EMERGENCY, RESCUE EQUIPMENT BREAKDOWN, BACK WASHING, CHEMICALS ADDED MANUALLY, CLEANING, ETC.	O.R.P. READINGS 12 HOUR BEFORE OPENING + 1X DURING THE DATE	
	WATER METER READINGS	
	MAKEUP WATER ADDED 20 L PER BATHER PER DAY	

POOL MAINTENANCE CHECKLIST

DATE		NUMBER OF DAYS SINCE LAST CHECK	

CHECK LIST	CHECKED?	NOTES / COMMENTS
CHECK FILTERS	○ YES ○ NO	
CHECK PUMPS	○ YES ○ NO	
CHECK WATER TEMPERATURE	○ YES ○ NO	WATER TEMPERATURE:
CHECK WATER LEVEL	○ YES ○ NO	AMOUNT OF WATER ADDED:
WATER TEST PH (IDEAL 7.4 - 7.6)	○ YES ○ NO	PH LEVEL:
WATER TEST CHLORINE (IDEAL 1.5 - 2.5)	○ YES ○ NO	CHLORINE LEVEL: HOW MUCH CHLORINE ADDED, IF APPLICABLE:
CLEAN AND CHECK SKIMMER BASKETS	○ YES ○ NO	
BRUSH SIDES	○ YES ○ NO	
LEAF SKIMMING	○ YES ○ NO	
VACUUM POOL	○ YES ○ NO	
CHECK YOUR STOCK OF POOL CHEMICALS	○ YES ○ NO	CHEMICALS / ITEMS PURCHASED:
CHECK YOUR FIRST AID SUPPLIES	○ YES ○ NO	ITEMS TO PURCHASE:
CHECK POOL SIDE ANY FENCES OR GATES	○ YES ○ NO	IF APPLICABLE, LIST MAINTENANCE REQUIRED:
OVERALL WATER CLARITY		

FUTHER NOTES / OBSERVATIONS

POOL DAILY INSPECTION RECORD

	SAT. / UNSAT.	TIME AM / PM	OPERATOR'S SIGNATURE		SAT. / UNSAT.	TIME AM / PM	OPERATOR'S SIGNATURE
EMERGENCY TELEPHONE 1/2 HOUR BEFORE OPENING				SPINEBOARD			
GROUND FAULT INTERRUPTER 1/2 HOUR BEFORE OPENING				FIRST AID KIT			
NON-CONDUCTING REACHING POLE				2 HEALTH WARNING SIGNS			
2 BUOYANT THROWING AIDS WITH ADEQUATE ROPE				UNSUPERVISED SIGN IF APPLICABLE			

POOL BI-HOURLY WATER TESTS

	1/2 HR BEFORE OPENING	TIME	TIME	TIME	TIME	TIME	TIME	TIME	TIME	TIME	TIME
	AM / PM	AM /PM	AM/PM	AM/PM	AM/PM	AM/PM	AM/PM	AM/PM	AM/PM	AM/PM	AM/PM
FREE AVAILABLE CHLORINE (F.A.C)											
TOTAL CHLORINE (T.C) / BROMINE											
COMBINE CHLORINE (T.C. - F.C.)											
PH (7.2 - 7.8)											
# OF BATHERS											
WATER CLARITY BLACK DISC VISIBLE FROM 9 METERS											
ALKALINITY MINIMUM 80 MG/L (1X / DAY)											
OPERATORS INITIALS											

RECORS OF ANY EMERGENCY, RESCUE EQUIPMENT BREAKDOWN, BACK WASHING, CHEMICALS ADDED MANUALLY, CLEANING, ETC.	O.R.P. READINGS 12 HOUR BEFORE OPENING + 1X DURING THE DATE	
	WATER METER READINGS	
	MAKEUP WATER ADDED 20 L PER BATHER PER DAY	

POOL MAINTENANCE CHECKLIST

DATE		NUMBER OF DAYS SINCE LAST CHECK	

CHECK LIST	CHECKED?	NOTES / COMMENTS
CHECK FILTERS	○ YES ○ NO	
CHECK PUMPS	○ YES ○ NO	
CHECK WATER TEMPERATURE	○ YES ○ NO	WATER TEMPERATURE:
CHECK WATER LEVEL	○ YES ○ NO	AMOUNT OF WATER ADDED:
WATER TEST PH (IDEAL 7.4 - 7.6)	○ YES ○ NO	PH LEVEL:
WATER TEST CHLORINE (IDEAL 1.5 - 2.5)	○ YES ○ NO	CHLORINE LEVEL: HOW MUCH CHLORINE ADDED, IF APPLICABLE:
CLEAN AND CHECK SKIMMER BASKETS	○ YES ○ NO	
BRUSH SIDES	○ YES ○ NO	
LEAF SKIMMING	○ YES ○ NO	
VACUUM POOL	○ YES ○ NO	
CHECK YOUR STOCK OF POOL CHEMICALS	○ YES ○ NO	CHEMICALS / ITEMS PURCHASED:
CHECK YOUR FIRST AID SUPPLIES	○ YES ○ NO	ITEMS TO PURCHASE:
CHECK POOL SIDE ANY FENCES OR GATES	○ YES ○ NO	IF APPLICABLE, LIST MAINTENANCE REQUIRED:
OVERALL WATER CLARITY		

FUTHER NOTES / OBSERVATIONS

POOL DAILY INSPECTION RECORD

	SAT. / UNSAT.	TIME AM / PM	OPERATOR'S SIGNATURE		SAT. / UNSAT.	TIME AM / PM	OPERATOR'S SIGNATURE
EMERGENCY TELEPHONE 1/2 HOUR BEFORE OPENING				SPINEBOARD			
GROUND FAULT INTER-RUPTER 1/2 HOUR BEFORE OPENING				FIRST AID KIT			
NON-CONDUCTING REACHING POLE				2 HEALTH WARNING SIGNS			
2 BUOYANT THROWING AIDS WITH ADEQUATE ROPE				UNSUPERVISED SIGN IF APPLICABLE			

POOL BI-HOURLY WATER TESTS

	1/2 HR BEFORE OPENING	TIME	TIME	TIME	TIME	TIME	TIME	TIME	TIME	TIME	TIME
	AM / PM	AM /PM	AM/PM	AM/PM	AM/PM	AM/PM	AM/PM	AM/PM	AM/PM	AM/PM	AM/PM
FREE AVAILABLE CHLORINE (F.A.C)											
TOTAL CHLORINE (T.C) / BROMINE											
COMBINE CHLORINE (T.C. - F.C.)											
PH (7.2 - 7.8)											
# OF BATHERS											
WATER CLARITY BLACK DISC VISIBLE FROM 9 METERS											
ALKALINITY MINIMUM 80 MG/L (1X / DAY)											
OPERATORS INITIALS											

RECORS OF ANY EMERGENCY, RESCUE EQUIPMENT BREAKDOWN, BACK WASHING, CHEMICALS ADDED MANUALLY, CLEANING, ETC.	O.R.P. READINGS 12 HOUR BEFORE OPENING + 1X DURING THE DATE	
	WATER METER READINGS	
	MAKEUP WATER ADDED 20 L PER BATHER PER DAY	

POOL MAINTENANCE CHECKLIST

DATE		NUMBER OF DAYS SINCE LAST CHECK	

CHECK LIST	CHECKED?	NOTES / COMMENTS
CHECK FILTERS	○ YES ○ NO	
CHECK PUMPS	○ YES ○ NO	
CHECK WATER TEMPERATURE	○ YES ○ NO	WATER TEMPERATURE:
CHECK WATER LEVEL	○ YES ○ NO	AMOUNT OF WATER ADDED:
WATER TEST PH (IDEAL 7.4 - 7.6)	○ YES ○ NO	PH LEVEL:
WATER TEST CHLORINE (IDEAL 1.5 - 2.5)	○ YES ○ NO	CHLORINE LEVEL: HOW MUCH CHLORINE ADDED, IF APPLICABLE:
CLEAN AND CHECK SKIMMER BASKETS	○ YES ○ NO	
BRUSH SIDES	○ YES ○ NO	
LEAF SKIMMING	○ YES ○ NO	
VACUUM POOL	○ YES ○ NO	
CHECK YOUR STOCK OF POOL CHEMICALS	○ YES ○ NO	CHEMICALS / ITEMS PURCHASED:
CHECK YOUR FIRST AID SUPPLIES	○ YES ○ NO	ITEMS TO PURCHASE:
CHECK POOL SIDE ANY FENCES OR GATES	○ YES ○ NO	IF APPLICABLE, LIST MAINTENANCE REQUIRED:
OVERALL WATER CLARITY		

FUTHER NOTES / OBSERVATIONS

POOL DAILY INSPECTION RECORD

	SAT. / UNSAT.	TIME AM / PM	OPERATOR'S SIGNATURE		SAT. / UNSAT.	TIME AM / PM	OPERATOR'S SIGNATURE
EMERGENCY TELEPHONE 1/2 HOUR BEFORE OPENING				SPINEBOARD			
GROUND FAULT INTERRUPTER 1/2 HOUR BEFORE OPENING				FIRST AID KIT			
NON-CONDUCTING REACHING POLE				2 HEALTH WARNING SIGNS			
2 BUOYANT THROWING AIDS WITH ADEQUATE ROPE				UNSUPERVISED SIGN IF APPLICABLE			

POOL BI-HOURLY WATER TESTS

	1/2 HR BEFORE OPENING	TIME	TIME	TIME	TIME	TIME	TIME	TIME	TIME	TIME	TIME	TIME
	AM / PM	AM /PM	AM/PM	AM/PM	AM/PM	AM/PM	AM/PM	AM/PM	AM/PM	AM/PM	AM/PM	AM/PM
FREE AVAILABLE CHLORINE (F.A.C)												
TOTAL CHLORINE (T.C) / BROMINE												
COMBINE CHLORINE (T.C. - F.C.)												
PH (7.2 - 7.8)												
# OF BATHERS												
WATER CLARITY BLACK DISC VISIBLE FROM 9 METERS												
ALKALINITY MINIMUM 80 MG/L (1X / DAY)												
OPERATORS INITIALS												

RECORS OF ANY EMERGENCY, RESCUE EQUIPMENT BREAKDOWN, BACK WASHING, CHEMICALS ADDED MANUALLY, CLEANING, ETC.	O.R.P. READINGS 12 HOUR BEFORE OPENING + 1X DURING THE DATE	
	WATER METER READINGS	
	MAKEUP WATER ADDED 20 L PER BATHER PER DAY	

POOL MAINTENANCE CHECKLIST

DATE		NUMBER OF DAYS SINCE LAST CHECK	

CHECK LIST	CHECKED?	NOTES / COMMENTS
CHECK FILTERS	○ YES ○ NO	
CHECK PUMPS	○ YES ○ NO	
CHECK WATER TEMPERATURE	○ YES ○ NO	WATER TEMPERATURE:
CHECK WATER LEVEL	○ YES ○ NO	AMOUNT OF WATER ADDED:
WATER TEST PH (IDEAL 7.4 - 7.6)	○ YES ○ NO	PH LEVEL:
WATER TEST CHLORINE (IDEAL 1.5 - 2.5)	○ YES ○ NO	CHLORINE LEVEL: HOW MUCH CHLORINE ADDED, IF APPLICABLE:
CLEAN AND CHECK SKIMMER BASKETS	○ YES ○ NO	
BRUSH SIDES	○ YES ○ NO	
LEAF SKIMMING	○ YES ○ NO	
VACUUM POOL	○ YES ○ NO	
CHECK YOUR STOCK OF POOL CHEMICALS	○ YES ○ NO	CHEMICALS / ITEMS PURCHASED:
CHECK YOUR FIRST AID SUPPLIES	○ YES ○ NO	ITEMS TO PURCHASE:
CHECK POOL SIDE ANY FENCES OR GATES	○ YES ○ NO	IF APPLICABLE, LIST MAINTENANCE REQUIRED:
OVERALL WATER CLARITY		

FUTHER NOTES / OBSERVATIONS

POOL DAILY INSPECTION RECORD

	SAT. / UNSAT.	TIME AM / PM	OPERATOR'S SIGNATURE		SAT. / UNSAT.	TIME AM / PM	OPERATOR'S SIGNATURE
EMERGENCY TELEPHONE 1/2 HOUR BEFORE OPENING				SPINEBOARD			
GROUND FAULT INTER- RUPTER 1/2 HOUR BEFORE OPENING				FIRST AID KIT			
NON-CONDUCTING REACH- ING POLE				2 HEALTH WARNING SIGNS			
2 BUOYANT THROWING AIDS WITH ADEQUATE ROPE				UNSUPERVISED SIGN IF APPLICABLE			

POOL BI-HOURLY WATER TESTS

	1/2 HR BEFORE OPENING	TIME	TIME	TIME	TIME	TIME	TIME	TIME	TIME	TIME	TIME	TIME
	AM / PM	AM/PM	AM/PM	AM/PM	AM/PM	AM/PM	AM/PM	AM/PM	AM/PM	AM/PM	AM/PM	AM/PM
FREE AVAILABLE CHLORINE (F.A.C)												
TOTAL CHLORINE (T.C) / BROMINE												
COMBINE CHLORINE (T.C. - F.C.)												
PH (7.2 - 7.8)												
# OF BATHERS												
WATER CLARITY BLACK DISC VISIBLE FROM 9 METERS												
ALKALINITY MINIMUM 80 MG/L (1X / DAY)												
OPERATORS INITIALS												

RECORS OF ANY EMERGENCY, RESCUE EQUIPMENT BREAKDOWN, BACK WASHING, CHEMICALS ADDED MANUALLY, CLEANING, ETC.	O.R.P. READINGS 12 HOUR BEFORE OPENING + 1X DURING THE DATE	
	WATER METER READINGS	
	MAKEUP WATER ADDED 20 L PER BATHER PER DAY	

POOL MAINTENANCE CHECKLIST

DATE		NUMBER OF DAYS SINCE LAST CHECK	

CHECK LIST	CHECKED?	NOTES / COMMENTS
CHECK FILTERS	○ YES ○ NO	
CHECK PUMPS	○ YES ○ NO	
CHECK WATER TEMPERATURE	○ YES ○ NO	WATER TEMPERATURE:
CHECK WATER LEVEL	○ YES ○ NO	AMOUNT OF WATER ADDED:
WATER TEST PH (IDEAL 7.4 - 7.6)	○ YES ○ NO	PH LEVEL:
WATER TEST CHLORINE (IDEAL 1.5 - 2.5)	○ YES ○ NO	CHLORINE LEVEL: HOW MUCH CHLORINE ADDED, IF APPLICABLE:
CLEAN AND CHECK SKIMMER BASKETS	○ YES ○ NO	
BRUSH SIDES	○ YES ○ NO	
LEAF SKIMMING	○ YES ○ NO	
VACUUM POOL	○ YES ○ NO	
CHECK YOUR STOCK OF POOL CHEMICALS	○ YES ○ NO	CHEMICALS / ITEMS PURCHASED:
CHECK YOUR FIRST AID SUPPLIES	○ YES ○ NO	ITEMS TO PURCHASE:
CHECK POOL SIDE ANY FENCES OR GATES	○ YES ○ NO	IF APPLICABLE, LIST MAINTENANCE REQUIRED:
OVERALL WATER CLARITY		

FUTHER NOTES / OBSERVATIONS

POOL DAILY INSPECTION RECORD

	SAT. / UNSAT.	TIME AM / PM	OPERATOR'S SIGNATURE		SAT. / UNSAT.	TIME AM / PM	OPERATOR'S SIGNATURE
EMERGENCY TELEPHONE 1/2 HOUR BEFORE OPENING				SPINEBOARD			
GROUND FAULT INTER-RUPTER 1/2 HOUR BEFORE OPENING				FIRST AID KIT			
NON-CONDUCTING REACH-ING POLE				2 HEALTH WARNING SIGNS			
2 BUOYANT THROWING AIDS WITH ADEQUATE ROPE				UNSUPERVISED SIGN IF APPLICABLE			

POOL BI-HOURLY WATER TESTS

	1/2 HR BEFORE OPENING	TIME	TIME	TIME	TIME	TIME	TIME	TIME	TIME	TIME	TIME
	AM / PM	AM /PM	AM/PM	AM/PM	AM/PM	AM/PM	AM/PM	AM/PM	AM/PM	AM/PM	AM/PM
FREE AVAILABLE CHLORINE (F.A.C)											
TOTAL CHLORINE (T.C) / BROMINE											
COMBINE CHLORINE (T.C. - F.C.)											
PH (7.2 - 7.8)											
# OF BATHERS											
WATER CLARITY BLACK DISC VISIBLE FROM 9 METERS											
ALKALINITY MINIMUM 80 MG/L (1X / DAY)											
OPERATORS INITIALS											

RECORS OF ANY EMERGENCY, RESCUE EQUIPMENT BREAKDOWN, BACK WASHING, CHEMICALS ADDED MANUALLY, CLEANING, ETC.	O.R.P. READINGS 12 HOUR BEFORE OPENING + 1X DURING THE DATE
	WATER METER READINGS
	MAKEUP WATER ADDED 20 L PER BATHER PER DAY

POOL MAINTENANCE CHECKLIST

DATE		NUMBER OF DAYS SINCE LAST CHECK	

CHECK LIST	CHECKED?	NOTES / COMMENTS
CHECK FILTERS	○ YES ○ NO	
CHECK PUMPS	○ YES ○ NO	
CHECK WATER TEMPERATURE	○ YES ○ NO	WATER TEMPERATURE:
CHECK WATER LEVEL	○ YES ○ NO	AMOUNT OF WATER ADDED:
WATER TEST PH (IDEAL 7.4 - 7.6)	○ YES ○ NO	PH LEVEL:
WATER TEST CHLORINE (IDEAL 1.5 - 2.5)	○ YES ○ NO	CHLORINE LEVEL: HOW MUCH CHLORINE ADDED, IF APPLICABLE:
CLEAN AND CHECK SKIMMER BASKETS	○ YES ○ NO	
BRUSH SIDES	○ YES ○ NO	
LEAF SKIMMING	○ YES ○ NO	
VACUUM POOL	○ YES ○ NO	
CHECK YOUR STOCK OF POOL CHEMICALS	○ YES ○ NO	CHEMICALS / ITEMS PURCHASED:
CHECK YOUR FIRST AID SUPPLIES	○ YES ○ NO	ITEMS TO PURCHASE:
CHECK POOL SIDE ANY FENCES OR GATES	○ YES ○ NO	IF APPLICABLE, LIST MAINTENANCE REQUIRED:
OVERALL WATER CLARITY		

FUTHER NOTES / OBSERVATIONS

POOL DAILY INSPECTION RECORD

	SAT. / UNSAT.	TIME AM / PM	OPERATOR'S SIGNATURE		SAT. / UNSAT.	TIME AM / PM	OPERATOR'S SIGNATURE
EMERGENCY TELEPHONE 1/2 HOUR BEFORE OPENING				SPINEBOARD			
GROUND FAULT INTER-RUPTER 1/2 HOUR BEFORE OPENING				FIRST AID KIT			
NON-CONDUCTING REACHING POLE				2 HEALTH WARNING SIGNS			
2 BUOYANT THROWING AIDS WITH ADEQUATE ROPE				UNSUPERVISED SIGN IF APPLICABLE			

POOL BI-HOURLY WATER TESTS

	1/2 HR BEFORE OPENING AM / PM	TIME AM/PM	TIME AM/PM	TIME AM/PM	TIME AM/PM	TIME AM/PM	TIME AM/PM	TIME AM/PM	TIME AM/PM	TIME AM/PM	TIME AM/PM
FREE AVAILABLE CHLORINE (F.A.C)											
TOTAL CHLORINE (T.C) / BROMINE											
COMBINE CHLORINE (T.C. - F.C.)											
PH (7.2 - 7.8)											
# OF BATHERS											
WATER CLARITY BLACK DISC VISIBLE FROM 9 METERS											
ALKALINITY MINIMUM 80 MG/L (1X / DAY)											
OPERATORS INITIALS											

RECORS OF ANY EMERGENCY, RESCUE EQUIPMENT BREAKDOWN, BACK WASHING, CHEMICALS ADDED MANUALLY, CLEANING, ETC.	O.R.P. READINGS 12 HOUR BEFORE OPENING + 1X DURING THE DATE
	WATER METER READINGS
	MAKEUP WATER ADDED 20 L PER BATHER PER DAY

POOL MAINTENANCE CHECKLIST

DATE		NUMBER OF DAYS SINCE LAST CHECK	

CHECK LIST	CHECKED?	NOTES / COMMENTS
CHECK FILTERS	○ YES ○ NO	
CHECK PUMPS	○ YES ○ NO	
CHECK WATER TEMPERATURE	○ YES ○ NO	WATER TEMPERATURE:
CHECK WATER LEVEL	○ YES ○ NO	AMOUNT OF WATER ADDED:
WATER TEST PH (IDEAL 7.4 - 7.6)	○ YES ○ NO	PH LEVEL:
WATER TEST CHLORINE (IDEAL 1.5 - 2.5)	○ YES ○ NO	CHLORINE LEVEL: HOW MUCH CHLORINE ADDED, IF APPLICABLE:
CLEAN AND CHECK SKIMMER BASKETS	○ YES ○ NO	
BRUSH SIDES	○ YES ○ NO	
LEAF SKIMMING	○ YES ○ NO	
VACUUM POOL	○ YES ○ NO	
CHECK YOUR STOCK OF POOL CHEMICALS	○ YES ○ NO	CHEMICALS / ITEMS PURCHASED:
CHECK YOUR FIRST AID SUPPLIES	○ YES ○ NO	ITEMS TO PURCHASE:
CHECK POOL SIDE ANY FENCES OR GATES	○ YES ○ NO	IF APPLICABLE, LIST MAINTENANCE REQUIRED:
OVERALL WATER CLARITY		

FUTHER NOTES / OBSERVATIONS

POOL DAILY INSPECTION RECORD

	SAT. / UNSAT.	TIME AM / PM	OPERATOR'S SIGNATURE		SAT. / UNSAT.	TIME AM / PM	OPERATOR'S SIGNATURE
EMERGENCY TELEPHONE 1/2 HOUR BEFORE OPENING				SPINEBOARD			
GROUND FAULT INTERRUPTER 1/2 HOUR BEFORE OPENING				FIRST AID KIT			
NON-CONDUCTING REACHING POLE				2 HEALTH WARNING SIGNS			
2 BUOYANT THROWING AIDS WITH ADEQUATE ROPE				UNSUPERVISED SIGN IF APPLICABLE			

POOL BI-HOURLY WATER TESTS

	1/2 HR BEFORE OPENING	TIME	TIME	TIME	TIME	TIME	TIME	TIME	TIME	TIME	TIME	TIME
	AM / PM	AM/PM	AM/PM	AM/PM	AM/PM	AM/PM	AM/PM	AM/PM	AM/PM	AM/PM	AM/PM	AM/PM
FREE AVAILABLE CHLORINE (F.A.C)												
TOTAL CHLORINE (T.C) / BROMINE												
COMBINE CHLORINE (T.C. - F.C.)												
PH (7.2 - 7.8)												
# OF BATHERS												
WATER CLARITY BLACK DISC VISIBLE FROM 9 METERS												
ALKALINITY MINIMUM 80 MG/L (1X / DAY)												
OPERATORS INITIALS												

RECORS OF ANY EMERGENCY, RESCUE EQUIPMENT BREAKDOWN, BACK WASHING, CHEMICALS ADDED MANUALLY, CLEANING, ETC.	O.R.P. READINGS 12 HOUR BEFORE OPENING + 1X DURING THE DATE	
	WATER METER READINGS	
	MAKEUP WATER ADDED 20 L PER BATHER PER DAY	

POOL MAINTENANCE CHECKLIST

DATE		NUMBER OF DAYS SINCE LAST CHECK	

CHECK LIST	CHECKED?	NOTES / COMMENTS
CHECK FILTERS	○ YES ○ NO	
CHECK PUMPS	○ YES ○ NO	
CHECK WATER TEMPERATURE	○ YES ○ NO	WATER TEMPERATURE:
CHECK WATER LEVEL	○ YES ○ NO	AMOUNT OF WATER ADDED:
WATER TEST PH (IDEAL 7.4 - 7.6)	○ YES ○ NO	PH LEVEL:
WATER TEST CHLORINE (IDEAL 1.5 - 2.5)	○ YES ○ NO	CHLORINE LEVEL: HOW MUCH CHLORINE ADDED, IF APPLICABLE:
CLEAN AND CHECK SKIMMER BASKETS	○ YES ○ NO	
BRUSH SIDES	○ YES ○ NO	
LEAF SKIMMING	○ YES ○ NO	
VACUUM POOL	○ YES ○ NO	
CHECK YOUR STOCK OF POOL CHEMICALS	○ YES ○ NO	CHEMICALS / ITEMS PURCHASED:
CHECK YOUR FIRST AID SUPPLIES	○ YES ○ NO	ITEMS TO PURCHASE:
CHECK POOL SIDE ANY FENCES OR GATES	○ YES ○ NO	IF APPLICABLE, LIST MAINTENANCE REQUIRED:
OVERALL WATER CLARITY		

FUTHER NOTES / OBSERVATIONS

POOL DAILY INSPECTION RECORD

	SAT. / UNSAT.	TIME AM / PM	OPERATOR'S SIGNATURE		SAT. / UNSAT.	TIME AM / PM	OPERATOR'S SIGNATURE
EMERGENCY TELEPHONE 1/2 HOUR BEFORE OPENING				SPINEBOARD			
GROUND FAULT INTERRUPTER 1/2 HOUR BEFORE OPENING				FIRST AID KIT			
NON-CONDUCTING REACHING POLE				2 HEALTH WARNING SIGNS			
2 BUOYANT THROWING AIDS WITH ADEQUATE ROPE				UNSUPERVISED SIGN IF APPLICABLE			

POOL BI-HOURLY WATER TESTS

	1/2 HR BEFORE OPENING AM / PM	TIME AM/PM	TIME AM/PM	TIME AM/PM	TIME AM/PM	TIME AM/PM	TIME AM/PM	TIME AM/PM	TIME AM/PM	TIME AM/PM	TIME AM/PM
FREE AVAILABLE CHLORINE (F.A.C)											
TOTAL CHLORINE (T.C) / BROMINE											
COMBINE CHLORINE (T.C - F.C.)											
PH (7.2 - 7.8)											
# OF BATHERS											
WATER CLARITY BLACK DISC VISIBLE FROM 9 METERS											
ALKALINITY MINIMUM 80 MG/L (1X / DAY)											
OPERATORS INITIALS											

RECORS OF ANY EMERGENCY, RESCUE EQUIPMENT BREAKDOWN, BACK WASHING, CHEMICALS ADDED MANUALLY, CLEANING, ETC.	O.R.P. READINGS 12 HOUR BEFORE OPENING + 1X DURING THE DATE	
	WATER METER READINGS	
	MAKEUP WATER ADDED 20 L PER BATHER PER DAY	

POOL MAINTENANCE CHECKLIST

DATE		NUMBER OF DAYS SINCE LAST CHECK	

CHECK LIST	CHECKED?	NOTES / COMMENTS
CHECK FILTERS	○ YES ○ NO	
CHECK PUMPS	○ YES ○ NO	
CHECK WATER TEMPERATURE	○ YES ○ NO	WATER TEMPERATURE:
CHECK WATER LEVEL	○ YES ○ NO	AMOUNT OF WATER ADDED:
WATER TEST PH (IDEAL 7.4 - 7.6)	○ YES ○ NO	PH LEVEL:
WATER TEST CHLORINE (IDEAL 1.5 - 2.5)	○ YES ○ NO	CHLORINE LEVEL: HOW MUCH CHLORINE ADDED, IF APPLICABLE:
CLEAN AND CHECK SKIMMER BASKETS	○ YES ○ NO	
BRUSH SIDES	○ YES ○ NO	
LEAF SKIMMING	○ YES ○ NO	
VACUUM POOL	○ YES ○ NO	
CHECK YOUR STOCK OF POOL CHEMICALS	○ YES ○ NO	CHEMICALS / ITEMS PURCHASED:
CHECK YOUR FIRST AID SUPPLIES	○ YES ○ NO	ITEMS TO PURCHASE:
CHECK POOL SIDE ANY FENCES OR GATES	○ YES ○ NO	IF APPLICABLE, LIST MAINTENANCE REQUIRED:
OVERALL WATER CLARITY		

FUTHER NOTES / OBSERVATIONS

POOL DAILY INSPECTION RECORD

	SAT. / UNSAT.	TIME AM / PM	OPERATOR'S SIGNATURE		SAT. / UNSAT.	TIME AM / PM	OPERATOR'S SIGNATURE
EMERGENCY TELEPHONE 1/2 HOUR BEFORE OPENING				SPINEBOARD			
GROUND FAULT INTERRUPTER 1/2 HOUR BEFORE OPENING				FIRST AID KIT			
NON-CONDUCTING REACHING POLE				2 HEALTH WARNING SIGNS			
2 BUOYANT THROWING AIDS WITH ADEQUATE ROPE				UNSUPERVISED SIGN IF APPLICABLE			

POOL BI-HOURLY WATER TESTS

	1/2 HR BEFORE OPENING	TIME	TIME	TIME	TIME	TIME	TIME	TIME	TIME	TIME	TIME	TIME
	AM / PM	AM /PM	AM/PM	AM/PM	AM/PM	AM/PM	AM/PM	AM/PM	AM/PM	AM/PM	AM/PM	AM/PM
FREE AVAILABLE CHLORINE (F.A.C)												
TOTAL CHLORINE (T.C) / BROMINE												
COMBINE CHLORINE (T.C. - F.C.)												
PH (7.2 - 7.8)												
# OF BATHERS												
WATER CLARITY BLACK DISC VISIBLE FROM 9 METERS												
ALKALINITY MINIMUM 80 MG/L (1X / DAY)												
OPERATORS INITIALS												

RECORS OF ANY EMERGENCY, RESCUE EQUIPMENT BREAKDOWN, BACK WASHING, CHEMICALS ADDED MANUALLY, CLEANING, ETC.	O.R.P. READINGS 12 HOUR BEFORE OPENING + 1X DURING THE DATE	
	WATER METER READINGS	
	MAKEUP WATER ADDED 20 L PER BATHER PER DAY	

POOL MAINTENANCE CHECKLIST

DATE		NUMBER OF DAYS SINCE LAST CHECK	

CHECK LIST	CHECKED?	NOTES / COMMENTS
CHECK FILTERS	○ YES ○ NO	
CHECK PUMPS	○ YES ○ NO	
CHECK WATER TEMPERATURE	○ YES ○ NO	WATER TEMPERATURE:
CHECK WATER LEVEL	○ YES ○ NO	AMOUNT OF WATER ADDED:
WATER TEST PH (IDEAL 7.4 - 7.6)	○ YES ○ NO	PH LEVEL:
WATER TEST CHLORINE (IDEAL 1.5 - 2.5)	○ YES ○ NO	CHLORINE LEVEL: HOW MUCH CHLORINE ADDED, IF APPLICABLE:
CLEAN AND CHECK SKIMMER BASKETS	○ YES ○ NO	
BRUSH SIDES	○ YES ○ NO	
LEAF SKIMMING	○ YES ○ NO	
VACUUM POOL	○ YES ○ NO	
CHECK YOUR STOCK OF POOL CHEMICALS	○ YES ○ NO	CHEMICALS / ITEMS PURCHASED:
CHECK YOUR FIRST AID SUPPLIES	○ YES ○ NO	ITEMS TO PURCHASE:
CHECK POOL SIDE ANY FENCES OR GATES	○ YES ○ NO	IF APPLICABLE, LIST MAINTENANCE REQUIRED:
OVERALL WATER CLARITY		

FUTHER NOTES / OBSERVATIONS

POOL DAILY INSPECTION RECORD

	SAT. / UNSAT.	TIME AM / PM	OPERATOR'S SIGNATURE		SAT. / UNSAT.	TIME AM / PM	OPERATOR'S SIGNATURE
EMERGENCY TELEPHONE 1/2 HOUR BEFORE OPENING				SPINEBOARD			
GROUND FAULT INTERRUPTER 1/2 HOUR BEFORE OPENING				FIRST AID KIT			
NON-CONDUCTING REACHING POLE				2 HEALTH WARNING SIGNS			
2 BUOYANT THROWING AIDS WITH ADEQUATE ROPE				UNSUPERVISED SIGN IF APPLICABLE			

POOL BI-HOURLY WATER TESTS

	1/2 HR BEFORE OPENING	TIME	TIME	TIME	TIME	TIME	TIME	TIME	TIME	TIME	TIME	TIME
	AM / PM	AM/PM	AM/PM	AM/PM	AM/PM	AM/PM	AM/PM	AM/PM	AM/PM	AM/PM	AM/PM	AM/PM
FREE AVAILABLE CHLORINE (F.A.C)												
TOTAL CHLORINE (T.C) / BROMINE												
COMBINE CHLORINE (T.C. - F.C.)												
PH (7.2 - 7.8)												
# OF BATHERS												
WATER CLARITY BLACK DISC VISIBLE FROM 9 METERS												
ALKALINITY MINIMUM 80 MG/L (1X / DAY)												
OPERATORS INITIALS												

RECORS OF ANY EMERGENCY, RESCUE EQUIPMENT BREAKDOWN, BACK WASHING, CHEMICALS ADDED MANUALLY, CLEANING, ETC.	O.R.P. READINGS 12 HOUR BEFORE OPENING + 1X DURING THE DATE
	WATER METER READINGS
	MAKEUP WATER ADDED 20 L PER BATHER PER DAY

POOL MAINTENANCE CHECKLIST

DATE		NUMBER OF DAYS SINCE LAST CHECK	

CHECK LIST	CHECKED?	NOTES / COMMENTS
CHECK FILTERS	○ YES ○ NO	
CHECK PUMPS	○ YES ○ NO	
CHECK WATER TEMPERATURE	○ YES ○ NO	WATER TEMPERATURE:
CHECK WATER LEVEL	○ YES ○ NO	AMOUNT OF WATER ADDED:
WATER TEST PH (IDEAL 7.4 - 7.6)	○ YES ○ NO	PH LEVEL:
WATER TEST CHLORINE (IDEAL 1.5 - 2.5)	○ YES ○ NO	CHLORINE LEVEL: HOW MUCH CHLORINE ADDED, IF APPLICABLE:
CLEAN AND CHECK SKIMMER BASKETS	○ YES ○ NO	
BRUSH SIDES	○ YES ○ NO	
LEAF SKIMMING	○ YES ○ NO	
VACUUM POOL	○ YES ○ NO	
CHECK YOUR STOCK OF POOL CHEMICALS	○ YES ○ NO	CHEMICALS / ITEMS PURCHASED:
CHECK YOUR FIRST AID SUPPLIES	○ YES ○ NO	ITEMS TO PURCHASE:
CHECK POOL SIDE ANY FENCES OR GATES	○ YES ○ NO	IF APPLICABLE, LIST MAINTENANCE REQUIRED:
OVERALL WATER CLARITY		

FUTHER NOTES / OBSERVATIONS

POOL DAILY INSPECTION RECORD

	SAT. / UNSAT.	TIME AM / PM	OPERATOR'S SIGNATURE		SAT. / UNSAT.	TIME AM / PM	OPERATOR'S SIGNATURE
EMERGENCY TELEPHONE 1/2 HOUR BEFORE OPENING				SPINEBOARD			
GROUND FAULT INTER-RUPTER 1/2 HOUR BEFORE OPENING				FIRST AID KIT			
NON-CONDUCTING REACH-ING POLE				2 HEALTH WARNING SIGNS			
2 BUOYANT THROWING AIDS WITH ADEQUATE ROPE				UNSUPERVISED SIGN IF APPLICABLE			

POOL BI-HOURLY WATER TESTS

	1/2 HR BEFORE OPENING	TIME	TIME	TIME	TIME	TIME	TIME	TIME	TIME	TIME	TIME	TIME
	AM / PM	AM /PM	AM/PM	AM/PM	AM/PM	AM/PM	AM/PM	AM/PM	AM/PM	AM/PM	AM/PM	AM/PM
FREE AVAILABLE CHLORINE (F.A.C)												
TOTAL CHLORINE (T.C) / BROMINE												
COMBINE CHLORINE (T.C. - F.C.)												
PH (7.2 - 7.8)												
# OF BATHERS												
WATER CLARITY BLACK DISC VISIBLE FROM 9 METERS												
ALKALINITY MINIMUM 80 MG/L (1X / DAY)												
OPERATORS INITIALS												

RECORS OF ANY EMERGENCY, RESCUE EQUIPMENT BREAKDOWN, BACK WASHING, CHEMICALS ADDED MANUALLY, CLEANING, ETC.	O.R.P. READINGS 12 HOUR BEFORE OPENING + 1X DURING THE DATE	
	WATER METER READINGS	
	MAKEUP WATER ADDED 20 L PER BATHER PER DAY	

POOL MAINTENANCE CHECKLIST

DATE		NUMBER OF DAYS SINCE LAST CHECK	

CHECK LIST	CHECKED?	NOTES / COMMENTS
CHECK FILTERS	○ YES ○ NO	
CHECK PUMPS	○ YES ○ NO	
CHECK WATER TEMPERATURE	○ YES ○ NO	WATER TEMPERATURE:
CHECK WATER LEVEL	○ YES ○ NO	AMOUNT OF WATER ADDED:
WATER TEST PH (IDEAL 7.4 - 7.6)	○ YES ○ NO	PH LEVEL:
WATER TEST CHLORINE (IDEAL 1.5 - 2.5)	○ YES ○ NO	CHLORINE LEVEL: HOW MUCH CHLORINE ADDED, IF APPLICABLE:
CLEAN AND CHECK SKIMMER BASKETS	○ YES ○ NO	
BRUSH SIDES	○ YES ○ NO	
LEAF SKIMMING	○ YES ○ NO	
VACUUM POOL	○ YES ○ NO	
CHECK YOUR STOCK OF POOL CHEMICALS	○ YES ○ NO	CHEMICALS / ITEMS PURCHASED:
CHECK YOUR FIRST AID SUPPLIES	○ YES ○ NO	ITEMS TO PURCHASE:
CHECK POOL SIDE ANY FENCES OR GATES	○ YES ○ NO	IF APPLICABLE, LIST MAINTENANCE REQUIRED:
OVERALL WATER CLARITY		

FUTHER NOTES / OBSERVATIONS

POOL DAILY INSPECTION RECORD

	SAT. / UNSAT.	TIME AM / PM	OPERATOR'S SIGNATURE		SAT. / UNSAT.	TIME AM / PM	OPERATOR'S SIGNATURE
EMERGENCY TELEPHONE 1/2 HOUR BEFORE OPENING				SPINEBOARD			
GROUND FAULT INTERRUPTER 1/2 HOUR BEFORE OPENING				FIRST AID KIT			
NON-CONDUCTING REACHING POLE				2 HEALTH WARNING SIGNS			
2 BUOYANT THROWING AIDS WITH ADEQUATE ROPE				UNSUPERVISED SIGN IF APPLICABLE			

POOL BI-HOURLY WATER TESTS

	1/2 HR BEFORE OPENING AM / PM	TIME AM/PM	TIME AM/PM	TIME AM/PM	TIME AM/PM	TIME AM/PM	TIME AM/PM	TIME AM/PM	TIME AM/PM	TIME AM/PM	TIME AM/PM	TIME AM/PM
FREE AVAILABLE CHLORINE (F.A.C)												
TOTAL CHLORINE (T.C) / BROMINE												
COMBINE CHLORINE (T.C. - F.C.)												
PH (7.2 - 7.8)												
# OF BATHERS												
WATER CLARITY BLACK DISC VISIBLE FROM 9 METERS												
ALKALINITY MINIMUM 80 MG/L (1X / DAY)												
OPERATORS INITIALS												

RECORS OF ANY EMERGENCY, RESCUE EQUIPMENT BREAKDOWN, BACK WASHING, CHEMICALS ADDED MANUALLY, CLEANING, ETC.	O.R.P. READINGS 12 HOUR BEFORE OPENING + 1X DURING THE DATE
	WATER METER READINGS
	MAKEUP WATER ADDED 20 L PER BATHER PER DAY

POOL MAINTENANCE CHECKLIST

DATE		NUMBER OF DAYS SINCE LAST CHECK	

CHECK LIST	CHECKED?	NOTES / COMMENTS
CHECK FILTERS	○ YES ○ NO	
CHECK PUMPS	○ YES ○ NO	
CHECK WATER TEMPERATURE	○ YES ○ NO	WATER TEMPERATURE:
CHECK WATER LEVEL	○ YES ○ NO	AMOUNT OF WATER ADDED:
WATER TEST PH (IDEAL 7.4 - 7.6)	○ YES ○ NO	PH LEVEL:
WATER TEST CHLORINE (IDEAL 1.5 - 2.5)	○ YES ○ NO	CHLORINE LEVEL: HOW MUCH CHLORINE ADDED, IF APPLICABLE:
CLEAN AND CHECK SKIMMER BASKETS	○ YES ○ NO	
BRUSH SIDES	○ YES ○ NO	
LEAF SKIMMING	○ YES ○ NO	
VACUUM POOL	○ YES ○ NO	
CHECK YOUR STOCK OF POOL CHEMICALS	○ YES ○ NO	CHEMICALS / ITEMS PURCHASED:
CHECK YOUR FIRST AID SUPPLIES	○ YES ○ NO	ITEMS TO PURCHASE:
CHECK POOL SIDE ANY FENCES OR GATES	○ YES ○ NO	IF APPLICABLE, LIST MAINTENANCE REQUIRED:
OVERALL WATER CLARITY		

FUTHER NOTES / OBSERVATIONS

POOL DAILY INSPECTION RECORD

	SAT. / UNSAT.	TIME AM / PM	OPERATOR'S SIGNATURE		SAT. / UNSAT.	TIME AM / PM	OPERATOR'S SIGNATURE
EMERGENCY TELEPHONE 1/2 HOUR BEFORE OPENING				SPINEBOARD			
GROUND FAULT INTERRUPTER 1/2 HOUR BEFORE OPENING				FIRST AID KIT			
NON-CONDUCTING REACHING POLE				2 HEALTH WARNING SIGNS			
2 BUOYANT THROWING AIDS WITH ADEQUATE ROPE				UNSUPERVISED SIGN IF APPLICABLE			

POOL BI-HOURLY WATER TESTS

	1/2 HR BEFORE OPENING	TIME	TIME	TIME	TIME	TIME	TIME	TIME	TIME	TIME	TIME	TIME
	AM / PM	AM/PM	AM/PM	AM/PM	AM/PM	AM/PM	AM/PM	AM/PM	AM/PM	AM/PM	AM/PM	AM/PM
FREE AVAILABLE CHLORINE (F.A.C)												
TOTAL CHLORINE (T.C) / BROMINE												
COMBINE CHLORINE (T.C. - F.C.)												
PH (7.2 - 7.8)												
# OF BATHERS												
WATER CLARITY BLACK DISC VISIBLE FROM 9 METERS												
ALKALINITY MINIMUM 80 MG/L (1X / DAY)												
OPERATORS INITIALS												

RECORS OF ANY EMERGENCY, RESCUE EQUIPMENT BREAKDOWN, BACK WASHING, CHEMICALS ADDED MANUALLY, CLEANING, ETC.	O.R.P. READINGS 12 HOUR BEFORE OPENING + 1X DURING THE DATE	
	WATER METER READINGS	
	MAKEUP WATER ADDED 20 L PER BATHER PER DAY	

POOL MAINTENANCE CHECKLIST

DATE		NUMBER OF DAYS SINCE LAST CHECK	

CHECK LIST	CHECKED?	NOTES / COMMENTS
CHECK FILTERS	○ YES ○ NO	
CHECK PUMPS	○ YES ○ NO	
CHECK WATER TEMPERATURE	○ YES ○ NO	WATER TEMPERATURE:
CHECK WATER LEVEL	○ YES ○ NO	AMOUNT OF WATER ADDED:
WATER TEST PH (IDEAL 7.4 - 7.6)	○ YES ○ NO	PH LEVEL:
WATER TEST CHLORINE (IDEAL 1.5 - 2.5)	○ YES ○ NO	CHLORINE LEVEL: HOW MUCH CHLORINE ADDED, IF APPLICABLE:
CLEAN AND CHECK SKIMMER BASKETS	○ YES ○ NO	
BRUSH SIDES	○ YES ○ NO	
LEAF SKIMMING	○ YES ○ NO	
VACUUM POOL	○ YES ○ NO	
CHECK YOUR STOCK OF POOL CHEMICALS	○ YES ○ NO	CHEMICALS / ITEMS PURCHASED:
CHECK YOUR FIRST AID SUPPLIES	○ YES ○ NO	ITEMS TO PURCHASE:
CHECK POOL SIDE ANY FENCES OR GATES	○ YES ○ NO	IF APPLICABLE, LIST MAINTENANCE REQUIRED:
OVERALL WATER CLARITY		

FUTHER NOTES / OBSERVATIONS

POOL DAILY INSPECTION RECORD

	SAT. / UNSAT.	TIME AM / PM	OPERATOR'S SIGNATURE		SAT. / UNSAT.	TIME AM / PM	OPERATOR'S SIGNATURE
EMERGENCY TELEPHONE 1/2 HOUR BEFORE OPENING				SPINEBOARD			
GROUND FAULT INTER-RUPTER 1/2 HOUR BEFORE OPENING				FIRST AID KIT			
NON-CONDUCTING REACHING POLE				2 HEALTH WARNING SIGNS			
2 BUOYANT THROWING AIDS WITH ADEQUATE ROPE				UNSUPERVISED SIGN IF APPLICABLE			

POOL BI-HOURLY WATER TESTS

	1/2 HR BEFORE OPENING	TIME	TIME	TIME	TIME	TIME	TIME	TIME	TIME	TIME	TIME	TIME
	AM / PM	AM /PM	AM/PM	AM/PM	AM/PM	AM/PM	AM/PM	AM/PM	AM/PM	AM/PM	AM/PM	AM/PM
FREE AVAILABLE CHLORINE (F.A.C)												
TOTAL CHLORINE (T.C) / BROMINE												
COMBINE CHLORINE (T.C. - F.C.)												
PH (7.2 - 7.8)												
# OF BATHERS												
WATER CLARITY BLACK DISC VISIBLE FROM 9 METERS												
ALKALINITY MINIMUM 80 MG/L (1X / DAY)												
OPERATORS INITIALS												

RECORS OF ANY EMERGENCY, RESCUE EQUIPMENT BREAKDOWN, BACK WASHING, CHEMICALS ADDED MANUALLY, CLEANING, ETC.	O.R.P. READINGS 12 HOUR BEFORE OPENING + 1X DURING THE DATE
	WATER METER READINGS
	MAKEUP WATER ADDED 20 L PER BATHER PER DAY

POOL MAINTENANCE CHECKLIST

DATE		NUMBER OF DAYS SINCE LAST CHECK	

CHECK LIST	CHECKED?	NOTES / COMMENTS
CHECK FILTERS	○ YES ○ NO	
CHECK PUMPS	○ YES ○ NO	
CHECK WATER TEMPERATURE	○ YES ○ NO	WATER TEMPERATURE:
CHECK WATER LEVEL	○ YES ○ NO	AMOUNT OF WATER ADDED:
WATER TEST PH (IDEAL 7.4 - 7.6)	○ YES ○ NO	PH LEVEL:
WATER TEST CHLORINE (IDEAL 1.5 - 2.5)	○ YES ○ NO	CHLORINE LEVEL: HOW MUCH CHLORINE ADDED, IF APPLICABLE:
CLEAN AND CHECK SKIMMER BASKETS	○ YES ○ NO	
BRUSH SIDES	○ YES ○ NO	
LEAF SKIMMING	○ YES ○ NO	
VACUUM POOL	○ YES ○ NO	
CHECK YOUR STOCK OF POOL CHEMICALS	○ YES ○ NO	CHEMICALS / ITEMS PURCHASED:
CHECK YOUR FIRST AID SUPPLIES	○ YES ○ NO	ITEMS TO PURCHASE:
CHECK POOL SIDE ANY FENCES OR GATES	○ YES ○ NO	IF APPLICABLE, LIST MAINTENANCE REQUIRED:
OVERALL WATER CLARITY		

FUTHER NOTES / OBSERVATIONS

POOL DAILY INSPECTION RECORD

	SAT. / UNSAT.	TIME AM / PM	OPERATOR'S SIGNATURE		SAT. / UNSAT.	TIME AM / PM	OPERATOR'S SIGNATURE
EMERGENCY TELEPHONE 1/2 HOUR BEFORE OPENING				SPINEBOARD			
GROUND FAULT INTERRUPTER 1/2 HOUR BEFORE OPENING				FIRST AID KIT			
NON-CONDUCTING REACHING POLE				2 HEALTH WARNING SIGNS			
2 BUOYANT THROWING AIDS WITH ADEQUATE ROPE				UNSUPERVISED SIGN IF APPLICABLE			

POOL BI-HOURLY WATER TESTS

	1/2 HR BEFORE OPENING	TIME	TIME	TIME	TIME	TIME	TIME	TIME	TIME	TIME	TIME	TIME
	AM / PM	AM/PM	AM/PM	AM/PM	AM/PM	AM/PM	AM/PM	AM/PM	AM/PM	AM/PM	AM/PM	AM/PM
FREE AVAILABLE CHLORINE (F.A.C)												
TOTAL CHLORINE (T.C) / BROMINE												
COMBINE CHLORINE (T.C. - F.C.)												
PH (7.2 - 7.8)												
# OF BATHERS												
WATER CLARITY BLACK DISC VISIBLE FROM 9 METERS												
ALKALINITY MINIMUM 80 MG/L (1X / DAY)												
OPERATORS INITIALS												

RECORS OF ANY EMERGENCY, RESCUE EQUIPMENT BREAKDOWN, BACK WASHING, CHEMICALS ADDED MANUALLY, CLEANING, ETC.	O.R.P. READINGS 12 HOUR BEFORE OPENING + 1X DURING THE DATE	
	WATER METER READINGS	
	MAKEUP WATER ADDED 20 L PER BATHER PER DAY	

POOL MAINTENANCE CHECKLIST

DATE		NUMBER OF DAYS SINCE LAST CHECK	

CHECK LIST	CHECKED?	NOTES / COMMENTS
CHECK FILTERS	○ YES ○ NO	
CHECK PUMPS	○ YES ○ NO	
CHECK WATER TEMPERATURE	○ YES ○ NO	WATER TEMPERATURE:
CHECK WATER LEVEL	○ YES ○ NO	AMOUNT OF WATER ADDED:
WATER TEST PH (IDEAL 7.4 - 7.6)	○ YES ○ NO	PH LEVEL:
WATER TEST CHLORINE (IDEAL 1.5 - 2.5)	○ YES ○ NO	CHLORINE LEVEL: HOW MUCH CHLORINE ADDED, IF APPLICABLE:
CLEAN AND CHECK SKIMMER BASKETS	○ YES ○ NO	
BRUSH SIDES	○ YES ○ NO	
LEAF SKIMMING	○ YES ○ NO	
VACUUM POOL	○ YES ○ NO	
CHECK YOUR STOCK OF POOL CHEMICALS	○ YES ○ NO	CHEMICALS / ITEMS PURCHASED:
CHECK YOUR FIRST AID SUPPLIES	○ YES ○ NO	ITEMS TO PURCHASE:
CHECK POOL SIDE ANY FENCES OR GATES	○ YES ○ NO	IF APPLICABLE, LIST MAINTENANCE REQUIRED:
OVERALL WATER CLARITY		

FUTHER NOTES / OBSERVATIONS

POOL DAILY INSPECTION RECORD

	SAT. / UNSAT.	TIME AM / PM	OPERATOR'S SIGNATURE		SAT. / UNSAT.	TIME AM / PM	OPERATOR'S SIGNATURE
EMERGENCY TELEPHONE 1/2 HOUR BEFORE OPENING				SPINEBOARD			
GROUND FAULT INTERRUPTER 1/2 HOUR BEFORE OPENING				FIRST AID KIT			
NON-CONDUCTING REACHING POLE				2 HEALTH WARNING SIGNS			
2 BUOYANT THROWING AIDS WITH ADEQUATE ROPE				UNSUPERVISED SIGN IF APPLICABLE			

POOL BI-HOURLY WATER TESTS

	1/2 HR BEFORE OPENING	TIME	TIME	TIME	TIME	TIME	TIME	TIME	TIME	TIME	TIME	TIME
	AM / PM	AM/PM	AM/PM	AM/PM	AM/PM	AM/PM	AM/PM	AM/PM	AM/PM	AM/PM	AM/PM	AM/PM
FREE AVAILABLE CHLORINE (F.A.C)												
TOTAL CHLORINE (T.C) / BROMINE												
COMBINE CHLORINE (T.C. - F.C.)												
PH (7.2 - 7.8)												
# OF BATHERS												
WATER CLARITY BLACK DISC VISIBLE FROM 9 METERS												
ALKALINITY MINIMUM 80 MG/L (1X / DAY)												
OPERATORS INITIALS												

RECORS OF ANY EMERGENCY, RESCUE EQUIPMENT BREAKDOWN, BACK WASHING, CHEMICALS ADDED MANUALLY, CLEANING, ETC.	O.R.P. READINGS 12 HOUR BEFORE OPENING + 1X DURING THE DATE	
	WATER METER READINGS	
	MAKEUP WATER ADDED 20 L PER BATHER PER DAY	

POOL MAINTENANCE CHECKLIST

DATE		NUMBER OF DAYS SINCE LAST CHECK	

CHECK LIST	CHECKED?	NOTES / COMMENTS
CHECK FILTERS	○ YES ○ NO	
CHECK PUMPS	○ YES ○ NO	
CHECK WATER TEMPERATURE	○ YES ○ NO	WATER TEMPERATURE:
CHECK WATER LEVEL	○ YES ○ NO	AMOUNT OF WATER ADDED:
WATER TEST PH (IDEAL 7.4 - 7.6)	○ YES ○ NO	PH LEVEL:
WATER TEST CHLORINE (IDEAL 1.5 - 2.5)	○ YES ○ NO	CHLORINE LEVEL: HOW MUCH CHLORINE ADDED, IF APPLICABLE:
CLEAN AND CHECK SKIMMER BASKETS	○ YES ○ NO	
BRUSH SIDES	○ YES ○ NO	
LEAF SKIMMING	○ YES ○ NO	
VACUUM POOL	○ YES ○ NO	
CHECK YOUR STOCK OF POOL CHEMICALS	○ YES ○ NO	CHEMICALS / ITEMS PURCHASED:
CHECK YOUR FIRST AID SUPPLIES	○ YES ○ NO	ITEMS TO PURCHASE:
CHECK POOL SIDE ANY FENCES OR GATES	○ YES ○ NO	IF APPLICABLE, LIST MAINTENANCE REQUIRED:
OVERALL WATER CLARITY		

FUTHER NOTES / OBSERVATIONS

POOL DAILY INSPECTION RECORD

	SAT. / UNSAT.	TIME AM / PM	OPERATOR'S SIGNATURE		SAT. / UNSAT.	TIME AM / PM	OPERATOR'S SIGNATURE
EMERGENCY TELEPHONE 1/2 HOUR BEFORE OPENING				SPINEBOARD			
GROUND FAULT INTER-RUPTER 1/2 HOUR BEFORE OPENING				FIRST AID KIT			
NON-CONDUCTING REACHING POLE				2 HEALTH WARNING SIGNS			
2 BUOYANT THROWING AIDS WITH ADEQUATE ROPE				UNSUPERVISED SIGN IF APPLICABLE			

POOL BI-HOURLY WATER TESTS

	1/2 HR BEFORE OPENING	TIME	TIME	TIME	TIME	TIME	TIME	TIME	TIME	TIME	TIME	TIME
	AM / PM	AM /PM	AM/PM	AM/PM	AM/PM	AM/PM	AM/PM	AM/PM	AM/PM	AM/PM	AM/PM	AM/PM
FREE AVAILABLE CHLORINE (F.A.C)												
TOTAL CHLORINE (T.C) / BROMINE												
COMBINE CHLORINE (T.C. - F.C.)												
PH (7.2 - 7.8)												
# OF BATHERS												
WATER CLARITY BLACK DISC VISIBLE FROM 9 METERS												
ALKALINITY MINIMUM 80 MG/L (1X / DAY)												
OPERATORS INITIALS												

RECORS OF ANY EMERGENCY, RESCUE EQUIPMENT BREAKDOWN, BACK WASHING, CHEMICALS ADDED MANUALLY, CLEANING, ETC.	O.R.P. READINGS 12 HOUR BEFORE OPENING + 1X DURING THE DATE	
	WATER METER READINGS	
	MAKEUP WATER ADDED 20 L PER BATHER PER DAY	

POOL MAINTENANCE CHECKLIST

DATE		NUMBER OF DAYS SINCE LAST CHECK	

CHECK LIST	CHECKED?	NOTES / COMMENTS
CHECK FILTERS	○ YES ○ NO	
CHECK PUMPS	○ YES ○ NO	
CHECK WATER TEMPERATURE	○ YES ○ NO	WATER TEMPERATURE:
CHECK WATER LEVEL	○ YES ○ NO	AMOUNT OF WATER ADDED:
WATER TEST PH (IDEAL 7.4 - 7.6)	○ YES ○ NO	PH LEVEL:
WATER TEST CHLORINE (IDEAL 1.5 - 2.5)	○ YES ○ NO	CHLORINE LEVEL: HOW MUCH CHLORINE ADDED, IF APPLICABLE:
CLEAN AND CHECK SKIMMER BASKETS	○ YES ○ NO	
BRUSH SIDES	○ YES ○ NO	
LEAF SKIMMING	○ YES ○ NO	
VACUUM POOL	○ YES ○ NO	
CHECK YOUR STOCK OF POOL CHEMICALS	○ YES ○ NO	CHEMICALS / ITEMS PURCHASED:
CHECK YOUR FIRST AID SUPPLIES	○ YES ○ NO	ITEMS TO PURCHASE:
CHECK POOL SIDE ANY FENCES OR GATES	○ YES ○ NO	IF APPLICABLE, LIST MAINTENANCE REQUIRED:
OVERALL WATER CLARITY		

FUTHER NOTES / OBSERVATIONS

POOL DAILY INSPECTION RECORD

	SAT. / UNSAT.	TIME AM / PM	OPERATOR'S SIGNATURE		SAT. / UNSAT.	TIME AM / PM	OPERATOR'S SIGNATURE
EMERGENCY TELEPHONE 1/2 HOUR BEFORE OPENING				SPINEBOARD			
GROUND FAULT INTERRUPTER 1/2 HOUR BEFORE OPENING				FIRST AID KIT			
NON-CONDUCTING REACHING POLE				2 HEALTH WARNING SIGNS			
2 BUOYANT THROWING AIDS WITH ADEQUATE ROPE				UNSUPERVISED SIGN IF APPLICABLE			

POOL BI-HOURLY WATER TESTS

	1/2 HR BEFORE OPENING	TIME	TIME	TIME	TIME	TIME	TIME	TIME	TIME	TIME	TIME
	AM / PM	AM /PM	AM/PM	AM/PM	AM/PM	AM/PM	AM/PM	AM/PM	AM/PM	AM/PM	AM/PM
FREE AVAILABLE CHLORINE (F.A.C)											
TOTAL CHLORINE (T.C) / BROMINE											
COMBINE CHLORINE (T.C. - F.C.)											
PH (7.2 - 7.8)											
# OF BATHERS											
WATER CLARITY BLACK DISC VISIBLE FROM 9 METERS											
ALKALINITY MINIMUM 80 MG/L (1X / DAY)											
OPERATORS INITIALS											

RECORS OF ANY EMERGENCY, RESCUE EQUIPMENT BREAKDOWN, BACK WASHING, CHEMICALS ADDED MANUALLY, CLEANING, ETC.	O.R.P. READINGS 12 HOUR BEFORE OPENING + 1X DURING THE DATE
	WATER METER READINGS
	MAKEUP WATER ADDED 20 L PER BATHER PER DAY

POOL MAINTENANCE CHECKLIST

DATE		NUMBER OF DAYS SINCE LAST CHECK	

CHECK LIST	CHECKED?	NOTES / COMMENTS
CHECK FILTERS	○ YES ○ NO	
CHECK PUMPS	○ YES ○ NO	
CHECK WATER TEMPERATURE	○ YES ○ NO	WATER TEMPERATURE:
CHECK WATER LEVEL	○ YES ○ NO	AMOUNT OF WATER ADDED:
WATER TEST PH (IDEAL 7.4 - 7.6)	○ YES ○ NO	PH LEVEL:
WATER TEST CHLORINE (IDEAL 1.5 - 2.5)	○ YES ○ NO	CHLORINE LEVEL: HOW MUCH CHLORINE ADDED, IF APPLICABLE:
CLEAN AND CHECK SKIMMER BASKETS	○ YES ○ NO	
BRUSH SIDES	○ YES ○ NO	
LEAF SKIMMING	○ YES ○ NO	
VACUUM POOL	○ YES ○ NO	
CHECK YOUR STOCK OF POOL CHEMICALS	○ YES ○ NO	CHEMICALS / ITEMS PURCHASED:
CHECK YOUR FIRST AID SUPPLIES	○ YES ○ NO	ITEMS TO PURCHASE:
CHECK POOL SIDE ANY FENCES OR GATES	○ YES ○ NO	IF APPLICABLE, LIST MAINTENANCE REQUIRED:
OVERALL WATER CLARITY		

FUTHER NOTES / OBSERVATIONS

POOL DAILY INSPECTION RECORD

	SAT. / UNSAT.	TIME AM / PM	OPERATOR'S SIGNATURE		SAT. / UNSAT.	TIME AM / PM	OPERATOR'S SIGNATURE
EMERGENCY TELEPHONE 1/2 HOUR BEFORE OPENING				SPINEBOARD			
GROUND FAULT INTERRUPTER 1/2 HOUR BEFORE OPENING				FIRST AID KIT			
NON-CONDUCTING REACHING POLE				2 HEALTH WARNING SIGNS			
2 BUOYANT THROWING AIDS WITH ADEQUATE ROPE				UNSUPERVISED SIGN IF APPLICABLE			

POOL BI-HOURLY WATER TESTS

	1/2 HR BEFORE OPENING	TIME	TIME	TIME	TIME	TIME	TIME	TIME	TIME	TIME	TIME	TIME
	AM / PM	AM/PM	AM/PM	AM/PM	AM/PM	AM/PM	AM/PM	AM/PM	AM/PM	AM/PM	AM/PM	AM/PM
FREE AVAILABLE CHLORINE (F.A.C)												
TOTAL CHLORINE (T.C) / BROMINE												
COMBINE CHLORINE (T.C. - F.C.)												
PH (7.2 - 7.8)												
# OF BATHERS												
WATER CLARITY BLACK DISC VISIBLE FROM 9 METERS												
ALKALINITY MINIMUM 80 MG/L (1X / DAY)												
OPERATORS INITIALS												

RECORS OF ANY EMERGENCY, RESCUE EQUIPMENT BREAKDOWN, BACK WASHING, CHEMICALS ADDED MANUALLY, CLEANING, ETC.	O.R.P. READINGS 12 HOUR BEFORE OPENING + 1X DURING THE DATE	
	WATER METER READINGS	
	MAKEUP WATER ADDED 20 L PER BATHER PER DAY	

POOL MAINTENANCE CHECKLIST

DATE		NUMBER OF DAYS SINCE LAST CHECK	

CHECK LIST	CHECKED?	NOTES / COMMENTS
CHECK FILTERS	○ YES ○ NO	
CHECK PUMPS	○ YES ○ NO	
CHECK WATER TEMPERATURE	○ YES ○ NO	WATER TEMPERATURE:
CHECK WATER LEVEL	○ YES ○ NO	AMOUNT OF WATER ADDED:
WATER TEST PH (IDEAL 7.4 - 7.6)	○ YES ○ NO	PH LEVEL:
WATER TEST CHLORINE (IDEAL 1.5 - 2.5)	○ YES ○ NO	CHLORINE LEVEL: HOW MUCH CHLORINE ADDED, IF APPLICABLE:
CLEAN AND CHECK SKIMMER BASKETS	○ YES ○ NO	
BRUSH SIDES	○ YES ○ NO	
LEAF SKIMMING	○ YES ○ NO	
VACUUM POOL	○ YES ○ NO	
CHECK YOUR STOCK OF POOL CHEMICALS	○ YES ○ NO	CHEMICALS / ITEMS PURCHASED:
CHECK YOUR FIRST AID SUPPLIES	○ YES ○ NO	ITEMS TO PURCHASE:
CHECK POOL SIDE ANY FENCES OR GATES	○ YES ○ NO	IF APPLICABLE, LIST MAINTENANCE REQUIRED:
OVERALL WATER CLARITY		

FUTHER NOTES / OBSERVATIONS

POOL DAILY INSPECTION RECORD

	SAT. / UNSAT.	TIME AM / PM	OPERATOR'S SIGNATURE		SAT. / UNSAT.	TIME AM / PM	OPERATOR'S SIGNATURE
EMERGENCY TELEPHONE 1/2 HOUR BEFORE OPENING				SPINEBOARD			
GROUND FAULT INTER-RUPTER 1/2 HOUR BEFORE OPENING				FIRST AID KIT			
NON-CONDUCTING REACH-ING POLE				2 HEALTH WARNING SIGNS			
2 BUOYANT THROWING AIDS WITH ADEQUATE ROPE				UNSUPERVISED SIGN IF APPLICABLE			

POOL BI-HOURLY WATER TESTS

	1/2 HR BEFORE OPENING	TIME	TIME	TIME	TIME	TIME	TIME	TIME	TIME	TIME	TIME	TIME
	AM / PM	AM/PM	AM/PM	AM/PM	AM/PM	AM/PM	AM/PM	AM/PM	AM/PM	AM/PM	AM/PM	AM/PM
FREE AVAILABLE CHLORINE (F.A.C)												
TOTAL CHLORINE (T.C) / BROMINE												
COMBINE CHLORINE (T.C. - F.C.)												
PH (7.2 - 7.8)												
# OF BATHERS												
WATER CLARITY BLACK DISC VISIBLE FROM 9 METERS												
ALKALINITY MINIMUM 80 MG/L (1X / DAY)												
OPERATORS INITIALS												

RECORS OF ANY EMERGENCY, RESCUE EQUIPMENT BREAKDOWN, BACK WASHING, CHEMICALS ADDED MANUALLY, CLEANING, ETC.	O.R.P. READINGS 12 HOUR BEFORE OPENING + 1X DURING THE DATE	
	WATER METER READINGS	
	MAKEUP WATER ADDED 20 L PER BATHER PER DAY	

POOL MAINTENANCE CHECKLIST

DATE		NUMBER OF DAYS SINCE LAST CHECK	

CHECK LIST	CHECKED?	NOTES / COMMENTS
CHECK FILTERS	○ YES ○ NO	
CHECK PUMPS	○ YES ○ NO	
CHECK WATER TEMPERATURE	○ YES ○ NO	WATER TEMPERATURE:
CHECK WATER LEVEL	○ YES ○ NO	AMOUNT OF WATER ADDED:
WATER TEST PH (IDEAL 7.4 - 7.6)	○ YES ○ NO	PH LEVEL:
WATER TEST CHLORINE (IDEAL 1.5 - 2.5)	○ YES ○ NO	CHLORINE LEVEL: HOW MUCH CHLORINE ADDED, IF APPLICABLE:
CLEAN AND CHECK SKIMMER BASKETS	○ YES ○ NO	
BRUSH SIDES	○ YES ○ NO	
LEAF SKIMMING	○ YES ○ NO	
VACUUM POOL	○ YES ○ NO	
CHECK YOUR STOCK OF POOL CHEMICALS	○ YES ○ NO	CHEMICALS / ITEMS PURCHASED:
CHECK YOUR FIRST AID SUPPLIES	○ YES ○ NO	ITEMS TO PURCHASE:
CHECK POOL SIDE ANY FENCES OR GATES	○ YES ○ NO	IF APPLICABLE, LIST MAINTENANCE REQUIRED:
OVERALL WATER CLARITY		

FUTHER NOTES / OBSERVATIONS

POOL DAILY INSPECTION RECORD

	SAT. / UNSAT.	TIME AM / PM	OPERATOR'S SIGNATURE		SAT. / UNSAT.	TIME AM / PM	OPERATOR'S SIGNATURE
EMERGENCY TELEPHONE 1/2 HOUR BEFORE OPENING				SPINEBOARD			
GROUND FAULT INTERRUPTER 1/2 HOUR BEFORE OPENING				FIRST AID KIT			
NON-CONDUCTING REACHING POLE				2 HEALTH WARNING SIGNS			
2 BUOYANT THROWING AIDS WITH ADEQUATE ROPE				UNSUPERVISED SIGN IF APPLICABLE			

POOL BI-HOURLY WATER TESTS

	1/2 HR BEFORE OPENING	TIME	TIME	TIME	TIME	TIME	TIME	TIME	TIME	TIME	TIME	TIME
	AM / PM	AM /PM	AM/PM	AM/PM	AM/PM	AM/PM	AM/PM	AM/PM	AM/PM	AM/PM	AM/PM	AM/PM
FREE AVAILABLE CHLORINE (F.A.C)												
TOTAL CHLORINE (T.C) / BROMINE												
COMBINE CHLORINE (T.C. - F.C.)												
PH (7.2 - 7.8)												
# OF BATHERS												
WATER CLARITY BLACK DISC VISIBLE FROM 9 METERS												
ALKALINITY MINIMUM 80 MG/L (1X / DAY)												
OPERATORS INITIALS												

RECORS OF ANY EMERGENCY, RESCUE EQUIPMENT BREAKDOWN, BACK WASHING, CHEMICALS ADDED MANUALLY, CLEANING, ETC.	O.R.P. READINGS 12 HOUR BEFORE OPENING + 1X DURING THE DATE	
	WATER METER READINGS	
	MAKEUP WATER ADDED 20 L PER BATHER PER DAY	

POOL MAINTENANCE CHECKLIST

DATE		NUMBER OF DAYS SINCE LAST CHECK	

CHECK LIST	CHECKED?	NOTES / COMMENTS
CHECK FILTERS	○ YES ○ NO	
CHECK PUMPS	○ YES ○ NO	
CHECK WATER TEMPERATURE	○ YES ○ NO	WATER TEMPERATURE:
CHECK WATER LEVEL	○ YES ○ NO	AMOUNT OF WATER ADDED:
WATER TEST PH (IDEAL 7.4 - 7.6)	○ YES ○ NO	PH LEVEL:
WATER TEST CHLORINE (IDEAL 1.5 - 2.5)	○ YES ○ NO	CHLORINE LEVEL: HOW MUCH CHLORINE ADDED, IF APPLICABLE:
CLEAN AND CHECK SKIMMER BASKETS	○ YES ○ NO	
BRUSH SIDES	○ YES ○ NO	
LEAF SKIMMING	○ YES ○ NO	
VACUUM POOL	○ YES ○ NO	
CHECK YOUR STOCK OF POOL CHEMICALS	○ YES ○ NO	CHEMICALS / ITEMS PURCHASED:
CHECK YOUR FIRST AID SUPPLIES	○ YES ○ NO	ITEMS TO PURCHASE:
CHECK POOL SIDE ANY FENCES OR GATES	○ YES ○ NO	IF APPLICABLE, LIST MAINTENANCE REQUIRED:
OVERALL WATER CLARITY		

FURTHER NOTES / OBSERVATIONS

POOL DAILY INSPECTION RECORD

	SAT. / UNSAT.	TIME AM / PM	OPERATOR'S SIGNATURE		SAT. / UNSAT.	TIME AM / PM	OPERATOR'S SIGNATURE
EMERGENCY TELEPHONE 1/2 HOUR BEFORE OPENING				SPINEBOARD			
GROUND FAULT INTER-RUPTER 1/2 HOUR BEFORE OPENING				FIRST AID KIT			
NON-CONDUCTING REACH-ING POLE				2 HEALTH WARNING SIGNS			
2 BUOYANT THROWING AIDS WITH ADEQUATE ROPE				UNSUPERVISED SIGN IF APPLICABLE			

POOL BI-HOURLY WATER TESTS

	1/2 HR BEFORE OPENING	TIME	TIME	TIME	TIME	TIME	TIME	TIME	TIME	TIME	TIME	TIME
	AM / PM	AM/PM	AM/PM	AM/PM	AM/PM	AM/PM	AM/PM	AM/PM	AM/PM	AM/PM	AM/PM	AM/PM
FREE AVAILABLE CHLORINE (F.A.C)												
TOTAL CHLORINE (T.C) / BROMINE												
COMBINE CHLORINE (T.C. - F.C.)												
PH (7.2 - 7.8)												
# OF BATHERS												
WATER CLARITY BLACK DISC VISIBLE FROM 9 METERS												
ALKALINITY MINIMUM 80 MG/L (1X / DAY)												
OPERATORS INITIALS												

RECORS OF ANY EMERGENCY, RESCUE EQUIPMENT BREAKDOWN, BACK WASHING, CHEMICALS ADDED MANUALLY, CLEANING, ETC.	O.R.P. READINGS 12 HOUR BEFORE OPENING + 1X DURING THE DATE	
	WATER METER READINGS	
	MAKEUP WATER ADDED 20 L PER BATHER PER DAY	

POOL MAINTENANCE CHECKLIST

DATE		NUMBER OF DAYS SINCE LAST CHECK	

CHECK LIST	CHECKED?	NOTES / COMMENTS
CHECK FILTERS	○ YES ○ NO	
CHECK PUMPS	○ YES ○ NO	
CHECK WATER TEMPERATURE	○ YES ○ NO	WATER TEMPERATURE:
CHECK WATER LEVEL	○ YES ○ NO	AMOUNT OF WATER ADDED:
WATER TEST PH (IDEAL 7.4 - 7.6)	○ YES ○ NO	PH LEVEL:
WATER TEST CHLORINE (IDEAL 1.5 - 2.5)	○ YES ○ NO	CHLORINE LEVEL: HOW MUCH CHLORINE ADDED, IF APPLICABLE:
CLEAN AND CHECK SKIMMER BASKETS	○ YES ○ NO	
BRUSH SIDES	○ YES ○ NO	
LEAF SKIMMING	○ YES ○ NO	
VACUUM POOL	○ YES ○ NO	
CHECK YOUR STOCK OF POOL CHEMICALS	○ YES ○ NO	CHEMICALS / ITEMS PURCHASED:
CHECK YOUR FIRST AID SUPPLIES	○ YES ○ NO	ITEMS TO PURCHASE:
CHECK POOL SIDE ANY FENCES OR GATES	○ YES ○ NO	IF APPLICABLE, LIST MAINTENANCE REQUIRED:
OVERALL WATER CLARITY		

FUTHER NOTES / OBSERVATIONS

POOL DAILY INSPECTION RECORD

	SAT. / UNSAT.	TIME AM / PM	OPERATOR'S SIGNATURE		SAT. / UNSAT.	TIME AM / PM	OPERATOR'S SIGNATURE
EMERGENCY TELEPHONE 1/2 HOUR BEFORE OPENING				SPINEBOARD			
GROUND FAULT INTERRUPTER 1/2 HOUR BEFORE OPENING				FIRST AID KIT			
NON-CONDUCTING REACHING POLE				2 HEALTH WARNING SIGNS			
2 BUOYANT THROWING AIDS WITH ADEQUATE ROPE				UNSUPERVISED SIGN IF APPLICABLE			

POOL BI-HOURLY WATER TESTS

	1/2 HR BEFORE OPENING	TIME	TIME	TIME	TIME	TIME	TIME	TIME	TIME	TIME	TIME
	AM / PM	AM/PM	AM/PM	AM/PM	AM/PM	AM/PM	AM/PM	AM/PM	AM/PM	AM/PM	AM/PM
FREE AVAILABLE CHLORINE (F.A.C)											
TOTAL CHLORINE (T.C) / BROMINE											
COMBINE CHLORINE (T.C. - F.C.)											
PH (7.2 - 7.8)											
# OF BATHERS											
WATER CLARITY BLACK DISC VISIBLE FROM 9 METERS											
ALKALINITY MINIMUM 80 MG/L (1X / DAY)											
OPERATORS INITIALS											

RECORS OF ANY EMERGENCY, RESCUE EQUIPMENT BREAKDOWN, BACK WASHING, CHEMICALS ADDED MANUALLY, CLEANING, ETC.	O.R.P. READINGS 12 HOUR BEFORE OPENING + 1X DURING THE DATE	
	WATER METER READINGS	
	MAKEUP WATER ADDED 20 L PER BATHER PER DAY	

www.ingramcontent.com/pod-product-compliance
Lightning Source LLC
Chambersburg PA
CBHW071407080526
44587CB00017B/3208